The Christian & Anger

Dealing with Life's Most Powerful Emotion

Charlie Avila

These chapters were first published in the *Spirit of Wisdom & Revelation* newsletters and in the teacherofthebible.com website in the United States.

Clovis Christian Center
3606 N. Fowler Ave
Fresno, California, USA 93727-1124

ISBN-10: **1985860643**
ISBN-13: **978-1985860643**
(Softcover Edition)

Printed in the United States

CONTENTS

DEDICATION

This book is dedicated to Pastor Rick and Dianne Avila. They are both the most faithful and loyal people I've ever met in the body of Christ. They are people of integrity who love the loss and disciple the found. They have encouraged, strengthened, and supported me in very simple and very profound ways. They are strong in faith, show agape love to all, and have a beautiful family. Thank you for your lives and committed service to King Jesus.

PREFACE

"Anger may be the most common emotional experience that human beings share," says Dr. Mark Cosgrove, in his excellent book, *Counseling for Anger*. Not all of us have been clinically depressed. Most of us have not experienced anorexia. But all of us have been angry. Some of us express anger every day. Most of us, if we are completely honest, have been angry recently.

The world is full of anger. As I write these words, there is an explosion of violence everywhere – suicide bombers, shootings at schools, riots in prison yards, massacres at churches, gang retaliations, domestic violence in homes, and political hostility. The list is very long. All of this violence is rooted in anger. People are angry. The truth is *Christians are angry.*

There is something else that is full of anger. The Bible is full of anger. There are many angry people in the Word of God. And there is a lot of instruction in the Bible on how to deal with our anger.

That is what this book is about. We go to God's Word and get God's wisdom on how to deal with this powerful emotion. From the very first pages of the Bible, all the way to its end, we find instruction on anger. *It is life's most powerful emotion.*

We start with Cain. God warned him that if he did not master anger, anger would master him. His anger exploded into violence when he killed his own brother, Abel, and shed his blood. The first man born on planet earth became a murderer. With Cain, you see that anger is a choice. You choose to be angry.

Next, we look at the angriest man in the Bible – Moses. From the beginning – when he killed an Egyptian – to his end – when he struck the rock – Moses was very angry. He became a murderer and he lost the Promised Land because he could not control his temper. With Moses, we see that anger is generational. Many of us are angry because we learned it from our fathers.

The most powerful instruction on anger comes from the lips of Jesus. In the Sermon on the Mount, He gives us a simple, but revealing, clue to the source of our anger problems. Jesus taught that anger is murder. It is "murder without knives." Just like we can commit adultery without the physical act, so we can commit murder without physically killing someone. With Jesus, we learn that the root of our anger problems is broken relationships. Many people have a life littered with broken relationships…and lots of anger.

Samson was the strongest man who ever lived, but he was weak in anger. He was also weak in his sexuality. Anger and Adultery – the two A's – go together. Most men have no idea how anger opens the door to sexual temptation. With Samson, we make the vital link between anger and sexual sin. Adulterers are angry people.

Jonah was a man who was enraged. Shockingly, he was angry at the mercy of God! When he was in trouble, he wanted mercy; when the Ninevites were in trouble, he wanted judgment. Angry people are critical and judgmental of others. Jonah was angry enough to die. With Jonah, we see that mercy and compassion diffuse our angry thoughts and ways.

The Apostle Paul was an angry man. He was angry before he met the Lord; and he battled anger after he met Him. He gave us a lot of important instruction on anger. He said anger is a work of the flesh and gives place to the devil. We must "put off anger." With Paul, we learn how to renew our minds so we can be transformed into the image of Him who created us.

Proverbs says more about anger than any other book of the Bible. The practical advice in this book shows us how to live day by day with ourselves and others. "A soft answer turns away anger, but a harsh word stirs it up." With Proverbs, we learn how to be "slow to anger."

Finally, we look at Ahithophel. He went from being an anointed counselor to a revengeful conspirator, all because of an anger that raged out of control. *He wanted to do to David what David had done to him.* With Ahithophel, you see that anger comes with revenge, and revenge is always deadly.

I have battled anger most of my adult life. This book was written in the crucible of life's experiences with friends, enemies, family, and churches. I share many personal stories of anger in this book. My prayer is that you will learn from my sins and be equipped to deal effectively with anger.

Jesus Christ is Lord. To God be the glory.
Charlie Avila, March 2018

1

Cain & Anger

"Cain was very angry, and his countenance fell."
(Genesis 4:5)

Anger is everywhere. Many people have not experienced being clinically depressed nor battled anorexia. Not all of us have been alcoholics nor have we all gambled at a casino. However, one thing is for sure – *all of us have expressed anger.* Some people have lived their entire lives dominated by angry responses. Some of the angriest people I know, including Christians, often deny that they have any problems with anger.

The Bible says a lot about anger, and that's because it is the most common, negative, emotional expression that anyone exhibits. From Genesis to Revelation, we see a lot of rage, fighting, strife, and even murder. There are many angry people in the Bible. The Bible offers us the most complete revelation on anger found anywhere. If you really want to understand anger in your life, you must study the Word of God carefully.

In this book, I want to look at many different aspects of anger from the lives of biblical personalities. In this first study, we'll look at Cain, because it offers so much insight into the subject and we can't afford to ignore what happened at the

1

beginning of human history. We'll also examine the life of Moses; a man who was plagued by anger issues all of his life. In the beginning, he was so angry that he murdered a man; in the end, he was so angry that he lost the Promised Land. When you look at his life, you see that anger is often passed generationally. I believe that the Book of Proverbs has more to say about anger than any other book, so we'll spend a whole chapter studying God's wisdom. We must look at Jonah, because we'll see in his life that anger is all about "rights." Jesus spoke about anger in the Sermon on the Mount, and He gives perhaps the most important instruction about the root causes of anger found anywhere in Scripture. Saul of Tarsus was a man who lived with a lot of rage when he was persecuting the church. As the apostle Paul, he wrote often about anger in his letters because I believe it was something he dealt with day by day. When we examine the life of David, Ahithophel, and Balaam, we'll see anger, revenge, and foolishness. Finally, Samson was a very powerful man physically. He could kill 1,000 men with a jawbone, tear off city gates, catch three hundred foxes, and rip apart a lion with his bare hands, but he could not control his hot temper. With Samson, we'll make the important connection between anger and sexual sin, and see how they work together to destroy men's lives. This will be an exciting study and we will all learn a lot about ourselves.

Anger in Families

The situation was tense. This husband and wife had reached the end of the rope. They wanted to talk to me, the Pastor. I scheduled an appointment with them to meet me at our church during the afternoon.

They had both been married before. They had children from other marriages and relationships. They now had several children together. The kids were wild and out of control. There was constant arguing and fighting. They both claimed to be Christians. I wasn't sure what I could do, but I was willing to listen to them and offer any advice that might help. I was hoping for the best and preparing for the worst.

As usual, when married people are mad at each other, they sit far apart in the room. Linda[1] sat on one side; Jim sat on the other. Linda started in right away. She laid out a long litany of complaints and grievances against her husband. It was one striking blow after another. No doubt, she had expressed these criticisms to him before. Perhaps family members, children, counselors, friends, and other Christians had heard this terrible list. She was methodical and deliberate. It was like a well-trained lawyer in a courtroom arguing each issue to convince the jury. She left no stone unturned. Every gory detail of his ugly life was divulged in this meeting. Years of pinned up frustration and anger were unleashed in short order.

Jim could hardly get in a word. He listened, but then he interjected when he disagreed. She always cut him off. "Let me finish!" she said. Then she plowed right into him again. The more she spoke, the more anger built up in the room. She got louder and louder. Then he started yelling back. I don't think they had any idea how loud and tense everything had become. I tried to interject to help calm things down, but it was all to no avail. I was actually concerned that things might turn physical right then and there. The truth of Proverbs 15:1 was played out right before me: "A harsh word stirs up anger."

After several angry exchanges, Linda had had enough. "Well, I'm done with you! It's over! I don't have one ounce of love for you. You're the worse man ever!" With that final statement, she pulled off her wedding ring and threw it at the table in the middle of the room. The gold ring just bounced off that table and landed somewhere on the carpet on the floor. She picked up her  belongings and walked out of the room. Jim and I just sat there in stunned silence. There really was nothing more to say. It was over. The "anger of man" had reached its ugly conclusion. Another failed marriage; more scattered kids; two former lovers are now angry enemies.

Within a few days, I received a call from Linda. "Can you meet me at the parking lot of such and such a store? I have

---

[1] The names have been changed to maintain confidentiality.

3

something that I need you to sign," she said. "Okay, I'll see you in a few minutes." When I got there, she pulled out paperwork for a restraining order. The order was to protect her from her husband, and she included my name on it to protect me (from him). "Sign it, and I will file it immediately." That was the last I ever saw of her.

Anger. There is so much anger in families. The prophet Micah wrote something that the Lord Jesus quoted later. He wrote, "For a son dishonors his father, a daughter rises up against her mother, a daughter-in-law against her mother-in-law – a man's enemies are the members of his own household."[2] Isn't that a sad history? The very ones we love the most, end up hating us. The opposition, disrespect, arguing, and strife generate a lot of anger in homes. There's lots of anger in our "own household."

Let's start with Cain. The first man born on planet earth was very angry. There was a lot of anger in the first family. In this story, the Lord teaches us that anger is a choice, and if we don't master anger, anger will master us.

Cain & Abel

The well-known story of Cain and Abel is found in Genesis, Chapter 4. They were Adam and Eve's first two children. Cain grew up to be a farmer and Abel a shepherd. The biblical narrative immediately takes us to a sacrifice made to the Lord. Cain offered "some of the fruits," "some of his harvest," or "part of the harvest," as various translations[3] word it. One commentator writes, "So Cain took some of what was left over and brought some of the fruit (produce) of the soil as an offering to the Lord. There is no indication that he brought the best or that he was wholeheartedly wanting to honor the Lord. He just brought from the fruit of the ground, whatever was available."[4]

When Abel offered the "firstborn" and the "fat" (finest, best) of "his flock," notice what it says at the end of verse 4, "The Lord respected (accepted, looked favorably upon) Abel and his

---

[2] See Micah 7:6 and Matthew 10:35-36.
[3] See the NIV, TEV, and CEV.
[4] *Genesis*, Stanley M. Horton, World Library Press, Inc., Springfield, Missouri, page 40.

offering." God accepted Abel before He accepted his offering. The Lord always looks first at the heart – the very character, nature, and spirit of a man – before He looks at his offering. We see this also in verse 5, "But He did not respect (accept) Cain and his offering." Cain's offering was rejected because his spirit was wrong. We'll examine this issue further a little later in this teaching.

In Genesis 4:5, we have the first mention in the Bible of "anger" or "angry." Cain expressed two powerful emotions so common to man. He was "very angry" and his "countenance fell." There is much to learn here so let's look at this closely.

The Hebrew adverb for "very" is "me'od." It means "vehemence" or "wholly." This adverb is often used in front of

words as an intensive or superlative. This is best described in Proverbs 29:11, "A fool gives full vent to his anger." Jonah expressed the same kind of anger when we read, "It displeased Jonah exceedingly, and he became very angry."[5] Cain was not just a little upset. He was giving full vent to his anger. Today we might call it "rage." Cain became enraged over what happened.

The Hebrew word for "angry" is "charah," and it means "to glow; to blaze up." This is a great description of anger – it makes us red-hot. We "glow" with anger. Cain was burning in anger. He became inflamed with it. The old KJV translation says that Cain was "very wroth." "Wroth" is an archaic English word that means "extremely angry."

We can't miss this point. Something further happened with Cain. He became depressed. Note how some translations word it: "His face fell," "he looked dejected," and "his face was downcast." We can't hide our feelings when it comes to depression. You could see depression on Cain's face. His countenance fell.

Doctors tell us that when we become angry, our adrenal glands secret a hormone that increases the speed and force of heart contraction. Our heart starts racing, our face turns red, and veins bulge out of our neck. However, when we come off that "high,"

---

[5] See Jonah 4:1.

our body goes to the other extreme. We crash, and we find ourselves tired and down in the dumps. We vacillate between anger and depression. So much depression is coming from anger.

The Lord Deals with Cain's Anger

How do you talk to a man when he's enraged? The Lord shows us how – you ask lots of questions, and then listen. He asked Cain three questions. In the first question, He addressed the anger. In the second question, He brings up the depression. Finally, the Lord shows Cain (and us) how to correct the anger problem.

Verse 6 reads, "So the LORD said to Cain, 'Why are you angry? And why has your countenance fallen?'" As we will see, Cain never answered either question. He had nothing to say. And note that Abel said nothing to Cain. The only one who speaks to Cain is the Lord.

Verse 7 is so critical to understanding anger that I cannot emphasize it enough. There is so much we can learn from this one verse. Please don't miss this.

The Lord will teach Cain how to deal with his anger. The NLT gives us the straightforward answer: "You will be accepted if you do what is right. But if you refuse to do what is right, then watch out!" Basically, the Lord told him, "The ball is in your court. It's your choice. If you'll just do what's right, I'll accept you." It really wasn't about Cain's offering. It was about his heart. His attitude was wrong. Notice that it doesn't say, "If your offering is right, then I'll accept your offering." No, it reads, "If YOU do well, will YOU not be accepted?"

Simply put, *anger is a choice. The reason many of us are angry right now is that we chose to be angry.* Abel didn't wrong Cain. The Lord was not unjust. It was Cain who was wrong. He chose to be angry and it was within his power to make it right. He could get out of this trap by doing what was right in God's sight.

Dr. Mark Cosgrove, in his excellent book, *Counseling for Anger*, makes this critical point: "Nothing makes people angry. People make themselves angry. If people are angry, it is because at their most fundamental level they have chosen to be angry. When I lose my temper, it is because I allow myself to explode along the behavior patterns dictated by my previous learning."[6] Mark it down – *Anger is a choice.* We chose to be angry. This is what the Lord is telling Cain. "It's up to you. You can do what's right, and I'll accept you. If you do what's wrong, things are going to get worse."

Do you remember what happened to King David? In 2 Samuel, Chapter 11, he saw a beautiful woman. He sent some of his servants to "take her" and bring her to his palace. He has sexual intercourse with her (commits adultery) and she becomes pregnant. He then concocts an elaborate scheme to murder Bathsheba's husband, Uriah. David arranges his death on the battlefield with the Lord's enemies. He commits adultery and murder in full view of God. What he did greatly displeased the Lord.

The Lord then sent David a prophet to expose his evil actions. In 2 Samuel 12:1-6, Nathan relates a story to David of "a rich man and a poor man." The rich man "had exceedingly many flocks and herds," while the poor man "had nothing but one little ewe lamb." This little lamb played with this poor man and his children in the fields and they watched over it with great love and tender care. The lamb even ate at the table with the family and the poor man treated it "like a daughter." However, one day, a traveler came to the rich man. In those days, Middle Eastern hospitality required that you provide shelter and food for a traveling friend. Rather than kill one of his many sheep and feed the man, the rich man took the only lamb that the poor man had and slaughtered it for the evening meal.

When David heard this story, his "anger was greatly aroused against the man." David even said, "The man who has done this shall surely die!" He adds, "This man has shown no pity (mercy)."

Then Nathan delivers the famous line that has thundered down the annals of human history – "You are the man!" David became enraged at the rich man in the story, not knowing that the rich man was him! *This is at the heart of so many angry men and women.* We are angry with ourselves; we chose to be angry; we're

---

[6] *Counseling for Anger,* Mark P. Cosgrove, Ph.D., Word Publishing, Dallas, TX, pages 45-46.

doing evil things in secret; and we express the anger at others! Others are not really making us angry; we're just angry people!

I'll never forget how the Lord dealt with me about my anger. Many years ago, we adopted a young boy who came from a very abused past. Daniel had many emotional, mental, and social issues to overcome. He always seemed to do the very things that displeased me. I would tell people words like this: "This little boy knows how to push my buttons; he does so many things that make me mad; Daniel is such a disobedient child and he really provokes me to anger." And with many other words, I complained to others about how my son made me angry.

One day the Lord got my attention on this issue. He said to me, "I didn't give you this child to make you angry; I gave him to you to reveal an angry man!" Wow, those words pierced my heart. *Other people do not create your spirit; they only reveal it.* Abel did not make Cain angry. Cain was simply an angry person. The rejection of Cain and his offering only revealed what was really inside of him.

I always remember the story told by a British Bible teacher. When he was about ten years old, he was walking home from school along a country road. He saw a big bull with two sharp horns lying down in an open field. The bull was casually chewing some grass and swatting flies off his body using his tail. This young boy thought the bull was just a mild-mannered animal that was relaxing on the grass. As young boys often do between school and home, he engaged in a little mischief. He found a rock by the side of the road and wondered what would happen if he threw it at the bull.

Little did he know what was going to happen. He threw that rock and it hit the bull right on the front of his head. For some reason, the bull stood up on his legs and began to swipe his legs/hooves along the ground and kick up some dust. The bull then charged the wooden fence that stood between that ten-year-old and the bull. The bull rammed into that fence with full force. Thank God, the fence did not give way. Obviously, the young boy ran for his dear life! He'd never seen such an angry bull.

The truth is that the rock did not make the bull mad; it only revealed an angry bull! *The rock only made what was really within come to the surface.* The wisest man who ever lived once said, "Do not be quickly provoked in your spirit, for anger resides (rests) in the bosom of fools."[7] Anger is "the fire within."

Looking at the Evil Within

What I'm going to teach now is very important. Let's try to answer the Lord's question to Cain – "Why are you so angry?" That would be a good question to ask yourself – *Why are you so angry? What's the source? Where is all the anger coming from?*

First, let's learn something about Cain from the New Testament. When the apostle John teaches about "loving your brother" and not "hating him," he brings up the story of Cain and Abel.[8] In 1 John 3:12, we have this powerful insight on Cain: "Don't love as Cain who was of the evil one and murdered his brother. *And why did he murder him? Because his works were evil and his brother's righteous.*" I've italicized the last two sentences. Did you hear what John said? He answers why Cain murdered Abel. It was because he belonged to "the evil one" (the devil) and "his works were evil."

So, let's see if we can follow this argument. Cain offers God what was evil and his lifestyle was evil. God does not accept Cain nor his offering. Cain becomes very angry and depressed. He takes out his anger and wrath on his brother. Let's boil it down to this – *Cain does what is evil and he gets angry with his brother.* He not only gets angry with him; he murders him. The Greek word for "murder" or "kill" in 1 John 3:12 is very strong. It means "to butcher; to slaughter; or to maim violently." In  fact, it is used repeatedly in the Book of Revelation to describe that Jesus was the "Lamb *slain* from the foundation of the world."[9] We know that Jesus shed a lot of blood from his head, back, side, wrists and feet. The cross of Jesus was a bloody event. The Bible

---

[7] See Ecclesiastes 7:9 in the NKJV and NIV translations.

[8] See 1 John 3:10-15.

[9] See verses like Revelation 5:6, 5:9, 5:12, and 13:8. The Greek word, "sphazō," is found only in 1 John and Revelation. So only the apostle John uses it in the New Testament.

also mentions the "blood of Abel" in several places.[10] We don't know specifically how Cain killed Abel, but we do know that blood was shed. He may have used a large rock, a sharp stick, or a metal instrument. Cain butchered or slaughtered Abel in a moment of angry rage! Maybe he stabbed him thirty times in his heart with a knife or crushed his skull with a rock.

The point I'm making is this: Cain was the one who was evil. Cain was wrong. Cain offered to God a sacrifice that was rejected. *And Cain was the one who had anger residing in his bosom.* He was not provoked. Abel is not the one to blame. The problem was internal, not external.

I think one of the most important teachings on anger is found in James 1:19-20. It reads, "My dear brothers, take note of this: Everyone should be quick to listen, slow to speak and slow to become angry, for man's anger does not bring about the righteous life that God desires." We're supposed to listen before we speak. We're supposed to be "slow to anger." Anger does not work the life that God desires. Anger will always take you down the wrong path.

Most of us stop at verse 20, but we must read the next verse. We must make the connection between verse 20 and verse 21. The next verse starts out with the all-important word, "Therefore." Therefore, because man's anger does not work God's righteousness, here is what you are to do. You are to "get rid of all the moral filth and evil in your lives." To get rid of anger in our heart, we must get rid of evil "in *our* lives!"

Here's the conclusion: *Many men are angry, but they are angry with themselves. They are angry because of secret sins in their own lives. They are angry because their lives don't seem to measure up. They live under law and under lots of condemnation. They are taking out their anger on loved ones in their home and at work.* Like Cain, we're killing the innocent ones around us.

When a Christian man sits at home viewing pornography on his computer for several hours, this is moral filth. This is evil. And anyone with even a little fear of the Lord in his life will be angry with himself. He will ask the Lord to forgive him, but then

---

[10] See Matthew 23:35, Luke 11:51, Hebrews 12:24, and Genesis 4:10-11.

he does it again the next week. The anger continues to build. He's angry at his lack of self-control. He's angry that he seems so weak and he can't overcome his sexual temptations. When this goes on week after week, month after month, year after year, you can bet that a lot of anger is building up within his soul. He is a ticking time bomb ready to explode. His wife and kids will experience his wrath. He will blame them for his anger problems. "They provoked me." "They make me mad." "They threw the rock at me." No, you are the bull. You are an angry man! You are taking it out on them so that the focus is moved away from you.

Anger as Master

Let's return to that critical verse, Genesis 4:7. In the second part of the verse, the Lord told Cain, "If you don't do what's right, sin (anger) is crouching at your door, and it's waiting to pounce on you, it desires you, it wants you, it's waiting to attack you and control your life." The CEV translation says, "Sin is waiting to attack you like a lion."  The Lord adds, but "you must master it," "you must overcome it," or "you must rule over it." The NLT says, "You must subdue it and be its master." *If you don't master anger, anger will master you.*

I'm reminded at this point of Paul's powerful words in Romans 6:12, 14, "Therefore do not let sin reign in your mortal body so that you obey its evil desires. For sin shall not be your master, because you are not under law, but under grace." Anger is a master. It is a cruel master. It dominates so many people. Even Christians can live with an "angry spirit" for many years. Proverbs 19:19 says, "A man of great wrath (anger) will suffer punishment; for if you rescue him, you will have to do it again." It's very difficult to break a man from his anger. If you deliver him once, you'll have to do it again…and again and again and again. And many of these men will live in denial of their anger.

I remember years ago a man in our church who was enraged. He told me that there were many times in his life that he would punch holes in doors or walls (including concrete) with such force that his family lived in stark terror of him. He was an angry man. Many times, he would "talk" to one of his grandkids at a party or outdoors or in church, and when he was only slightly upset, he would yell with a deep, angry tone. For him, this was normal. I have found that many angry people have deep voices. They are loud!

I also remember a Christian lady that endured many, many years of physical abuse from her husband. She held in a lot of anger and rage. It was so interesting working with her, because she would argue with others about anything and everything. Every simple conversation turned into a controversy and she would get hot! After years of enduring this, people finally had to tell her, "You have a problem with anger." She immediately denied it. She would go talk to all of her friends at work, and ask them, "Do you think I'm an angry person?" Of course, all of them agreed with her. She would come back to people and announce, "You see, no one thinks that I have an anger problem. You're judging me or you don't really understand me. I don't have an anger problem." By the way, she could yell too. When she got mad, her voice was very high and her facial expressions were contorted.

Many women who have been molested when young or physically abused by men are enraged. Only the grace of Jesus and the power of the Holy Spirit can heal them. I find that anger becomes so much a part of their personalities that they no longer see it as strange but normal.

The apostle Paul warned us in Ephesians 4:26-27, "And don't sin by letting anger control you. Don't let the sun go down while you are still angry, for anger gives a foothold to the devil." When we chose anger, and stay angry, and give full vent to our anger, it will control us. And the devil will be given an open door into our life. He will take advantage of us and work his evil destruction in our family and friends. Don't let the sun go down on your anger. Deal with it before the day is out. Get before the Lord. Cry out for help from the Holy Spirit who is the Comforter. The grace of God delivers us from the works of the flesh.

Remember, anger is a choice. We can choose to be angry or not. If you continually give way to anger, anger will slowly begin to master or control your life. It will become so much a part of who you are that it becomes part of your personality. I can say this much: You will have to work on it diligently if you want to get it out of your life (at least where it's not dominating and controlling how you react).

Anger & Murder

When people wanted to talk about murder, Jesus said let's talk about anger. In Matthew 5:21-26, He explains that those who are angry are "in danger of judgment." Anger, when taken to its extreme, results in murder. It is not difficult to see that every murder that has happened on earth, started with anger in the heart.

The Federal Bureau of Investigation (FBI) keeps national statistics on many crimes including violent ones. They report that over 80% of all murders are committed among family members. As we said earlier, there is a lot of anger in families. Such was the case with Cain in Genesis.

Cain came up with a plan to get Abel alone in the field. As I understand it, there were only two other people around (Adam and Eve). Possibly there were daughters born that are not listed in the Genesis account. Nevertheless, Cain rose up against Abel, attacked him, and killed him in the field.

In verse 9, the Lord asked Cain, "Where is your brother?" Of course, God was not seeking information. He knew exactly where Abel was buried or left for dead. He was confronting Cain with his murder. Truly, his anger had overcome and mastered him.

I believe we can hear the cynical tone of Cain's voice in verse 9. Cain lies right to God's face. He says, "I don't know," and adds the mocking and derisive question, "Am I my brother's keeper?" I can just picture Cain telling the Lord with contempt and ridicule, "Oh, so You expect me to take care of him? What do I look like, a babysitter?" His anger led to murder. His murder led to lying. Now he's a mocker and cynic. Anger's ugly roots have spread throughout Cain's heart. Anger is now his lord and master.

Cain's anger brought about the Lord's curse. God curses Cain to a life as a fugitive, vagabond, and "restless wanderer." Worst of all, Cain was driven from the "presence of the Lord." This last action by God drove him to self-pity and despair.

Concluding Thoughts

Anger is a strong beast that seeks to control our lives. If we don't master anger, anger will master us. Anger is a choice – we chose to be angry. So many people who are depressed are really very angry. If we are to effectively deal with the anger that burns within, we must deal with the evil in our lives. Don't let anger ruin your family, marriage, children, and work. In the power of the Holy Spirit, and by the grace of God, declare war against this work of the flesh. Anger will not rule over you because you are not under law but under grace.

In the next chapter, we will look at the life of one of the greatest leaders of all time. Moses was a man of great abilities, but he had one defining weakness – anger. It controlled most of his life. The Bible talks about his anger more than any other person. The trials and hardships of leading millions of Jews to the Promised Land brought out the worst in him. He expressed his anger repeatedly when the children of Israel rebelled against God and him. The truth is his ancestor, Levi, brought the curse of anger into his family line. Moses looked just like his distant relative. "Like father, like son." We will study how anger was passed from one generation to another in the tribe of Levi.

YouTube Videos:
- **The Christian and Anger 01a**
- **The Christian and Anger 01b**

2

Moses & Anger

*"Then Moses, hot with anger, left Pharaoh." "And
Moses was very angry with them." "So Moses'
anger became hot, and he cast the tablets out of his
hands and broke them at the foot of the mountain."
(Exodus 11:8, 16:20, 32:19)*

Moses was very angry. Many things quickly provoked him. In fact, the Bible mentions his anger more than any other person. He was angry with Pharaoh. He was angry with his brother Aaron. He was angry with Eleazar and Ithamar. He was angry at the Israelites. He was angry with his cousin Korah. He was angry with the officers and captains of the  army. He was so angry with an Egyptian, that he murdered him and buried him in the sand. At the end of his life, he became enraged at the Israelites, struck the rock twice, and it cost him the Promised Land.

Why would a man so mightily used by God struggle so much with anger? I strongly believe that his anger was generational. There was lots of anger in his family line. He learned to do what his ancestors had done. And the truth is there is a lot of that type of anger seen in families today. I have seen anger learned and passed on from one generation to another. Only in Christ, can the curses be broken.

Angry Responses Can Be Learned

Proverbs 22:24-25 are two very important verses regarding anger and its curses. It reads, "Make no friendship with an angry man, and with a furious (hot-tempered) man do not go, lest you learn his ways and get a snare for your soul." We are not to have any association with a person who has a hot, violent temper. Why? God's wisdom gives us two reasons: 1) You will learn his ways and 2) you will get a snare in your soul. The NCV translation says, "If you do, you will be like them. Then you will be in real danger." The NLT says, "You will learn to be like them and endanger your soul." An angry person will teach you how to respond to difficult situations with anger. You are going to learn his bad habits. Then the writer adds this frightening thought – it will cause a noose to be put around your soul. The Hebrew word for "snare" is the one used for capturing an animal by putting a noose around its neck. The only problem is this noose doesn't go around your neck, but around your soul! "Soul" (nephesh) basically means your very breath.

Proverbs 22:24-25 might be easy to obey if the "angry man" or "furious man" is your neighbor or a distant friend, but what if it's your dad? What if it's your mom who lives in your house? How can you escape the bad influence of a parent that you have to live with day after day? What happens if your family line for many generations has been filled with anger? I have seen this "generational anger" in many families in local churches. And what do you think happens in families who have used that anger to physically abuse wives and children, or homes where absentee fathers have opened the doors to sexual abuse from boyfriends and uncles? In cases of molestation and incest, you will see real rage. I believe this is the case with Moses. His family line displayed enormous rage and anger over a molestation (rape). It brought a violent response from Moses' great-grandfather, Levi. Let's trace this cruel family history and see how anger dominates lives.

16

Levi & His Anger

Something terrible happened in Genesis, Chapter 34. A young lady was raped. A man named "Shechem" ended up forcing himself on "Dinah," the daughter of Jacob and Leah. The whole chapter details the awful event and the horrific aftermath. It tells us that Dinah was "defiled" and "violated."[11] There is something else that this chapter clearly describes – some people became very, very angry.

The story goes like this: After Shechem raped Dinah, for some twisted reason, he wanted to marry her. He convinced his dad, Hamor, to talk to Jacob, Dinah's father, to arrange a marriage which included a dowry. Shechem "loved" Dinah so much that he was willing to pay any price to get her.

Unfortunately for Shechem, his rape really enraged two of Dinah's brothers, Simeon and Levi. They deceitfully plotted a scheme whereby all the men of Hamor's clan would take circumcision as the only requirement for intermarrying with Jacob's "tribe." The unsuspecting men of the town agreed with Hamor and Shechem and were circumcised. While they were recovering from this painful procedure, Simeon and Levi took up their swords "and came boldly upon the city and killed all the males. They killed Hamor and Shechem his son with the edge of the sword, and took Dinah from Shechem's house." Simeon and Levi even "plundered" all the wealth, livestock, wives, and children of this city. They committed this extreme act of violence because "their sister had been defiled."

Jacob was shocked and sickened by the brutal and vicious action of his sons. What kind of scene was left by Simeon and Levi who attacked an entire city with swords when they were so vulnerable? Even after slaughtering many men, they still had the audacity to plunder innocent women and "little children." No wonder Jacob feared that "the inhabitants of the land," including the "Canaanites and Perizzites," would rise up against him and his family and "destroy my household and I." What a terrible chapter in the first book of the Bible!

---

[11] See Genesis 34:2, 34:5, 34:13, and 34:27.

Cursed be their Anger!

Jacob never forgot the barbaric act of his two sons. At the end of his life, when it came time to speak blessings over his twelve sons, Jacob cursed Simeon and Levi. Genesis 49:5-7 reveal the ominous words: "Simeon and Levi are brothers; instruments of cruelty are in their dwelling place. Let me not enter their council, let me not join their assembly, for they have killed men in their anger and hamstrung oxen as they pleased. Cursed be their anger, so fierce, and their fury, so cruel! I will scatter them in Jacob and disperse them in Israel." One translation of verse 6 ends with "For in their anger they murdered men, and they crippled oxen just for sport." They were sick!

Jacob pronounced a curse over Simeon and Levi because of their violent temper. As with many people in the Bible, curses always have devastating effects on future generations.

Moses' family tree is amazingly detailed. There are seven different sections of Scripture that give us his exact family line. Levi was his great-grandfather. Levi had three sons – Gershon, Kohath, and Merari.[12] He had at least one daughter, Jochebed, who was Moses' mother.[13] Kohath had four sons – Amram, Izhar, Hebron, and Uzziel.[14] Amram, Levi's grandson, married Jochebed, Levi's daughter. They had three famous children – Aaron, Moses, and Miriam.

So let's review: Levi begat Kohath; Kohath begat Amram; and Amram begat Moses.

Exodus 2:1 reads, "And a man of the house of Levi went and took as wife a daughter of Levi." This was the beginning of Moses' life – he had a double-portion of anger passed from Levi.

Think about this for just one minute. Jochebed was Moses' mom. Recall that it was "Pharaoh's daughter" who

---

[12] See Genesis 46:11; Exodus 6:16; Numbers 3:17, 26:57; 1 Chronicles 6:1, 6:16, and 23:6.

[13] See Exodus 2:1, 6:20; Numbers 26:59. In Exodus 2:1, Jochebed is called "a daughter of Levi;" in Exodus 6:20, "his father's (Kohath) sister;" and in Numbers 26:59, "Amram's wife was Jochebed daughter of Levi."

[14] See Exodus 6:18, Numbers 3:19, 3:27, 26:58; 1 Chronicles 6:2, 6:18, 23:12, and 26:23.

assigned Jochebed the task of raising Moses for her. Jochebed was Levi's daughter. Ponder this: Her dad is a mass-murderer. He, along with his brother, had killed many men with the "edge of the sword." Also, her father uses a sword to cut the tendons on the legs of animals (like oxen) in order to maim and cripple them. Your father's temper is so violent, that even his father (Jacob) pronounces a curse on his anger. I think Jochebed grew up in a very dark and sick home. What is more, Amram is Levi's grandson, so he's part of the family curse. Amram's dad, Kohath, was also raised in Levi's home. Based on Proverbs 22:24-25, I'm positive that a lot of anger was passed on to Moses from his parents.

It took no time for his anger to be expressed in a very destructive way. When Moses saw an "Egyptian beating a Hebrew, one of his brethren," he took immediate action. Exodus 2:12 says, "So Moses looked this way and that way, and when he saw no one, he killed the Egyptian and hid him in the sand." Like Cain before him, Moses let his anger lead to murder. When he was discovered, he fled Egypt for Midian.

Moses & Anger

One commentator said this about anger: "The more power a man wields, the more destructive his anger can be."[15] This was true in the life of Moses. Moses the Lawgiver had anger deeply rooted in his heart and in his family line. More often than not, that anger cannot come to the surface until it gets under pressure or the fire of difficult situations. Moses was constantly put under very trying circumstances that brought his anger in full view of everyone.

Silver and gold cannot be refined unless it is put in a hot, melting furnace where the impurities ("scum") come to the surface. It is only then that the impurities can be removed and what is left is silver/gold that is purer and more valuable.

Let's look at five events in Moses' life that sorely tried his patience and provoked him to anger. While I think Moses was a

---

[15] *Proverbs*, Kenneth T. Aitken, The Daily Study Bible Series, The Westminster Press, Philadelphia, page 108.

man "easily angered," these circumstances would really test *any* man's patience.

Before a Stubborn Pharaoh: Anyone who reads the story of the ten plagues in Exodus, Chapters 5-12, will be quickly exasperated with the hardness of Pharaoh's heart and the Lord's slow, methodical destruction of Egypt and its gods. If I were God, I would have gotten rid of Pharaoh after the first plague and delivered the Israelites immediately! However, God's ways and thoughts are much higher and better than ours.

Moses was so frustrated with the angry responses of the Israelites and Pharaoh, that at several points he wanted to call it quits. In one moment of desperation, Moses told the Lord, "My own people (Israel) won't listen to me; how can I expect Pharaoh to listen to me? Besides, I'm a terrible speaker with faltering and stammering speech!"[16] There's nothing more frustrating for a leader than when no one is listening to you! Moses was fed up!

Over and over, ad nauseam, Moses endured these words, "Pharaoh hardened his heart" or "the Lord hardened Pharaoh's heart." How long, O Lord? After nine plagues, Moses had reached the end of his patience. So often, the Lord will take us to a point where we can no longer endure. Our spirit is irritated and vexed. We're done. Then the Lord graciously steps in. Finally, after nine terrible plagues that nearly destroyed all of Egypt, the Lord tells Moses that there is one more devastating plague that will cause Pharaoh to release God's people.[17]

Moses, in a fiery rage, announces the death of the firstborn throughout Egypt. When Moses delivers the dreadful news to Pharaoh, Exodus 11:8 tells us, "Then Moses went out from Pharaoh in great anger." Not "anger," but "great anger." He was hot! The Hebrew word here for "great" is "choriy," which means, "intense; burning."

What about you? Have you dealt with stubborn people in your family or at work? Have you seen anger rise to the surface in your life? Once again, you really don't know what's deep down

---

[16] See Exodus 6:12.

[17] Even so, Pharaoh was such a hard-hearted man that he pursued the Israelites after they left Egypt.

in your soul until just the right person or situation arises that draws out the hidden anger in your life.

I have seen my share of "stubborn Pharaohs" in my short lifetime. I remember a man who came to our church years ago. I failed to investigate his background before I put him into leadership. I found out years later, from a ministry leader in another part of town, that he had caused lots of trouble in their ministry because of his stubbornness.

Nevertheless, I saw him as a very zealous person for the things of the Lord. Unfortunately, he was quite overbearing and he angered several people. One time, he angered a man (husband) so much because of how he talked to his wife, that this man left our church. This man who left – I found out later – was a very angry and violent man himself! He called me and told me, "You will be sorry that you ever put this guy in leadership! He's sick!" With that comment, he hung up the phone.

Within a few months, I saw what he meant. This man was starting to have regular, heated arguments with his wife. He began to treat people at church in disrespectful ways. Finally, I sat him down and talked to him about his out-of-control life. This short chat only made him angrier! He blew up and walked out of the church building. Regrettably, he didn't actually leave the church. I had to replace him in leadership, but he continued to attend the services…and he was hot! I can't tell you how difficult it is to preach on Sunday morning with an angry person staring you down while you preach! After one Sunday, he confronted me in the back of the church and chewed me out! Oh, what fun it is to be a Pastor!

Well, you can believe that this brought out an unbelievable amount of anger in me. The truth is I was not aware that I was capable of such anger. He continued to attend our church for about six more weeks. Finally, like Moses, I could take it no more. I asked him to leave and not return. When he left, he made it his personal mission to badmouth me around town. This only infuriated me more. Now I was really hot. At one point, several months later, I had to confess to the Lord that I actually hated the guy! I was humbled before the Lord and I saw first-hand how strong my flesh really was. I was so disappointed in my actions, but I began to face the ugly monster of anger in my life for the first time. God sent this angry man to reveal some real shortcomings in my life.

Manna that Turns to Worms and Stinks: Exodus 16:20 says, "However, they (Israelites) paid no attention to Moses; they kept part of the manna until morning, but it bred worms (maggots) and began to stink. Moses was very angry with them."

Right after the Lord supernaturally delivered the Israelites from Egypt through the Red Sea (Exodus 14), God's people were singing "the song of Moses" and dancing for joy (Exodus 15). Suddenly, the mood changes drastically from rejoicing to complaining (Exodus 16). How is God going to feed millions of Jews and animals in a howling wilderness? Despite their murmurings, the Lord graciously provides quail in the evenings and manna in the mornings. He truly is Jehovah-Jireh, the Lord Who Provides, and nothing is impossible for Him!

The Lord required a little work from them though. Actually, it was a simple act of daily faith in the Lord's provision.

Whenever they went to get the manna, they could not keep any of it stored away in their tents. "Each man had gathered according to each one's need." "Some gathered more, some gathered less."[18] In other words, only get what you need for that day. Don't waste any manna. Pick up enough "daily bread" and no more. Moses' conclusion was "let no one leave any manna till morning."[19]

The people did not listen to Moses' simple instruction. They disobeyed the clear teaching of their spiritual leader. The disobedient Israelites soon felt the ire of Moses. And when Moses told them to get twice as much on Friday so they could rest on Saturday, people still went looking for manna on Saturday. Moses was ready to pull out his hair and theirs!

Nothing will test a person's patience nor incite anger like disobedience. This is especially true of parents with their children

---

[18] See Exodus 16:16-19.

[19] Interestingly, when they gathered on Friday, they could keep the manna through Saturday and it did not bred worms nor did it spoil. This was a weekly, supernatural act of God that allowed them to obey the Sabbath, the day of rest.

and pastors with their members. Lamentably, some of my most angry outbursts have come at home when my kids disobeyed me. I don't like being disobeyed. I've also displayed angry responses to disobedient sheep that paid no attention to their shepherd.

As a pastor, I don't have problems developing a sermon for Sunday morning. I don't have a problem making tough financial decisions for the good of the church. I actually enjoy counseling people through marriage problems and other crises. However, one of the most trying times for me is when Christians are disobedient to the Lord and to me as a local pastor. A pastor feels useless when people don't walk in the ways of the Lord. And in these last days when stubborn people will challenge and defy authority, we need the power of the Holy Spirit to restrain our tempers.

Such was the case when I dealt with Sam[20] many years ago. Sam and his wife, Joanne, were faithful members of our local church. They had been married nearly forty-five years. They were very generous givers. They told everyone about the blessings of tithing and giving offerings to support the work of the Lord. Moreover, Sam was very evangelistic. He told everyone about the Lord at his place of employment. He was a manager and he used his influence to witness to many.

Somehow, Sam slowly became cold in his relationship with Jesus. Little by little, he lost his zeal. His Bible reading and prayer life had dwindled down to nothing. It wasn't long before he started missing church services on a regular basis. He had an excuse ready for each Sunday. It was no surprise that he was soon going to serve the flesh, the world, or the devil.

One Sunday, I was preaching a message from Proverbs Chapter 6, on the seven things that God hates (abominations). I felt like it was a convicting message. As soon as the service was over, Sam came straight to the front of the church sanctuary and said, "Boy, that was a very negative message. I came to church to be lifted up and encouraged, and here you are talking about things that God hates. I'm leaving this service very discouraged." Of course, I felt bad. Maybe I missed the Lord. Maybe I should be

---

[20] The names have been changed to protect people's confidentiality.

preaching more encouraging messages. I too left the church discouraged and confused.

Sometime during the middle of that week, Sam called me. "I need to talk to you right away. Are you at the church?" "Yes," I told him. "I'll be right over," he said. Since he lived nearby, he was at the church office in about fifteen minutes.

"I need to tell you something very serious, Pastor Charlie. Promise me that you won't tell anyone." "What happened?" I asked. "I'm having an affair with a younger woman. She's only thirty-two." Sam had recently turned seventy years of age. The moment he told me this secret, I thought about his dear wife, Joanne. She had been a very faithful wife. In recent years, she had struggled with many health issues. She was a person who loved the Lord and cared deeply about other people, especially those who were hurting.

I'm not sure why, but I was so angry with Sam that I actually stood up and walked away from him and into the sanctuary. I turned around and said, "Sam, you need to get out of this relationship immediately, repent, and get right with the Lord! You are playing with fire! Have you told Joanne? Does she know?" I found out later that she knew all about the affair from the gossip that was circulating through the neighborhood.

I couldn't shake this scandal from my mind. It stayed with me day after day. I thought about what Jesus said to the Ephesian church when He spoke to them about "leaving your first love. Remember the height from which you have fallen!"[21] I thought about how far Sam had fallen. A man who once shared the light was now living in darkness!

I called him every week. I was very angry with him. I told him in very strong words, "Break off that adulterous relationship! You are rebelling against the Lord and bringing unforeseen curses into your life!" He gave me an excuse every time. He knew how I felt about these things and he continued in his ungodly lifestyle. I felt disrespected and dishonored.

About three weeks into this conversation, I felt a note of seriousness from the Lord about his situation. I began to sense that he was in a lot of danger. I needed to make sure that I was

---

[21] See Revelation 2:4-6.

24

hearing from the Lord and not just my anger, so I decided to fast and pray for him. I remembered the verse in Deuteronomy where Moses wrote, "And the Lord was very angry with Aaron and would have destroyed him; so I prayed for Aaron."[22] I prayed for Sam.

After a season of prayer, and in the midst of my anger, the Lord gave me a stern warning for him. "Repent or else," the Lord said. "If he doesn't repent soon, something terrible is going to happen in his life." I called him up and asked him to come over to the church building. I was very nervous about how he would receive the word from the Lord. I paced up and down the sanctuary for a long time.

When Sam walked into the church sanctuary, he sat in the same place from where he first told me about the affair. I asked him, "Do you believe that God speaks to people? Do you think that he speaks to me, your pastor?" He said, "Yes. Did He tell you anything?" "Yes, but I don't think you want to hear it. I have a very serious warning for you from God." He got very quiet and put his head down. I tried to calm down, but I was hot!

"The Lord told me that if you don't break off this adulterous relationship immediately that something terrible was going to happen to you. I even want to tell you that your life is in danger, but the Lord didn't give me that kind of detail. Mark my words: You are in serious trouble with the Lord. He has shown you great kindness and mercy, and now you are disobeying Him and doing something that He hates. No wonder you didn't like what I was preaching from Proverbs Chapter 6!"

Incredibly, he still made several excuses. He just could not break away from his adulteress. I was startled that he would defy the Lord in this way. Beyond the shock, my blood pressure was up and my heart was still very agitated. The anger was gnawing away at my spirit.

I said, "I hope nothing bad happens to you, but you've put yourself in a very dangerous position. I'll keep praying for you." With that, he left.

Within about ten days, I received a frantic phone call from Sam at 6:30 in the morning. "Pastor! Pastor! Please come over

---

[22] See Deuteronomy 9:20.

to my house. The paramedics are here. They found Joanne on the floor of the bathroom. They can't revive her. They just told me that she's dead! Can you come over right now?!"

Wow! I left my house right away and drove about twenty minutes to his house. When I got there, the paramedics were still there. He was nervously smoking a cigarette in the kitchen. I saw that his hands were trembling. I was allowed to walk into the bedroom and then into the bathroom. There was Joanne's body on the floor covered with a white sheet. It was over. She was dead. A feeling of numbness came over me. I thought I was living in a dream world. Sam's wife of forty-five years was gone. She was a dear personal friend of my wife and me. I was in a state of grief.

What do I say to Sam? Actually, I said very little. The truth is there was little to say. I had already said what I needed to say ten days earlier. Now, it was too late. The devastating reality of God's words washed over my soul. God is serious. God is not playing games. God demands obedience from His children.

Dear friends, we will all go through difficult trials in life. We have all been disobedient. I hated what happened to Sam. It struck me odd that the person who was innocent, the woman who was serving the Lord and walking in His ways, was the very one that died that day. The logic made no sense. Sam commits adultery; Joanne dies. The sad reality is that as I write this article today, both Sam and his girlfriend are still living together in adultery. No amount of judgment changed his mind.

God let me see a lot of anger in my heart that I didn't even know was there. To this day, I pray for Sam and help him from time to time when he calls me. He is as confused as ever. I've learned a little bit more about God's abounding grace where sin abounds. The whole experience humbled me and gave me an appreciation of just how much God suffers with His children.

The Golden Calf and Dancing: Nothing brought out Moses' anger like the incident with the golden calf. It is safe to say that Moses was enraged.

I'm going to write something now that perhaps some people will disagree with, but I have seen its truth played out in several difficult situations. *I believe one of the main reasons why*

Moses was so angry was because the Lord was "very angry." While the story of the golden calf is found in Exodus Chapter 32, Moses would write many years later, at the end of his life, that "the Lord was angry enough with you to have destroyed you," "you provoked Him to anger," "I was afraid of the anger and hot displeasure with which the Lord was angry with you, to destroy you," and "the Lord was very angry with Aaron and would have destroyed him."[23] That's a lot of anger. What Moses felt in the spiritual realm from the Lord was stirring up his own strong emotions.

When Moses came down from the mountain with two tablets of stone in his hands, he saw an incredible scene of debauchery, rebellion and self-indulgence. It was unrestrained wildness. Exodus 32:19-20 reads, "When Moses approached the camp and saw the calf and the dancing, his anger burned and he threw the tablets out of his hands, breaking them to pieces at the foot of the mountain. And he took the calf they had made and burned it in the fire; then he ground it to powder, scattered it on the water and made  the Israelites drink it." Breaking tablets, grinding the calf down, making the Israelites drink from that filthy water...wow, Moses was burning with anger! One translation says, "Moses' anger became hot." Aaron, his brother, would say a few verses later, "Do not let the anger of my lord become hot."

Because of the golden calf and the surrounding immorality and unruliness, 3,000 people were killed. And guess what? It was the Levites who rose up with swords (sound familiar? Remember Levi and his sword?) The descendants of Levi killed these thousands in the judgment of God. What a violent scene!

This is a very deep question. It is one that we will try to address from time to time in this book. Just how does a godly person handle injustice? Where are the limits and boundaries on anger when you see blatant rebellion and injustice? Where do we draw the line? Does a Christian really handle "righteous anger" well? That's a difficult question. My personal thought is that

---

[23] See Deuteronomy 9:8-20.

most of us don't handle anger well, righteous or not. When we give full vent to our anger, it causes lots of turmoil and trouble.

What do you do with people who are disobeying the very first commandment that Moses was receiving on top of the mountain? What do you do when the very glory of God is burning the mountain and the Israelites can see with physical eyes the awesomeness of God; yet, they still treat Him with contempt and open rebellion? A few counselors and Christian authors have written that righteous anger is a very normal part of life. I understand that, but I don't think we handle it with God's grace and wisdom. Things easily get out of hand. I've seen churches torn apart by "righteous anger." More on this topic later. Let's talk about another personal story.

She was a very intelligent, witty, and beautiful young lady. She was a young Christian and very friendly with people. She had everything going for her…or so it appeared.

Karen had a problem. She always seemed to pick the wrong men to be her "boyfriends." The only way I can say it straight is that *she always picked losers*. A woman like her could have the cream of the crop; but it seemed like she went down to the worst part of town and picked the most undesirable man. Why? It frustrated (and angered) me to no end. I have seen this situation time after time.[24]

She ended up marrying a young guy who was in and out of drugs and could never hold down a job. I counseled him many times, but nothing in his life ever changed. It seemed like he changed jobs once or twice a month. The jobs he would get were always dead-end jobs. There was no way that he could maintain a family with his employment history.

To make a long story short, she caught him in multiple affairs and finally divorced him. Her parents were devastated, but not really surprised, by all that was happening to their lovely daughter. It was a depressing and discouraging situation.

---

[24] While I don't understand every situation, I have often seen that these women have a very, very low view of themselves. They don't think they are good enough, pretty enough, or worthy enough for a nice guy. Many times, these women have been abused or they have a poor relationship with their father.

I sat down with the family one day at their home and talked with them about what had just happened. We meet again at the church to talk further about her predicament. We all concluded that before she "selected" another guy, she needed to talk to her parents and me before making any final decisions. I personally didn't like the arrangement, because I didn't want that kind of control over people's lives. Everyone has to work out his own salvation with fear and trembling. Nevertheless, I made myself available in the event they needed my counsel.

Well, one day, Karen continued with her old ways. She started dating a guy who just got out of jail. I saw the guy at a local amusement park, and his body was covered with tattoos and he looked like a street gang member. On one Sunday, she even brought him to one of our church services. We found out within one week that this young man had cut off the GPS[25] tag off of his ankle. He was actually a fugitive, running away from law enforcement. And Karen was driving him around town to help him with his errands! We told her, "Don't you realize that you could be arrested too? You are helping a fugitive get around town." This time I wanted to scream! What are you doing?! I noticed that I was getting pretty angry.

Miraculously, she finally left that guy and we sat down and talked to her again. For some reason, she just wasn't getting it. Her parents were very frustrated. Fortunately, she repented, and continued to come to church. We put her through a process of restoration and discipleship so she could serve once again in our church. She took some Bible classes, served in the worship ministry, and helped out in the children's church. Things were looking up (and I cooled down!).

Unbeknownst to us, there was a new scheme brewing secretly in her life. Her younger brother was in jail for a drug violation. While in prison, he showed a picture of his cute sister to a gang member who shared his cell. This gang-banger saw that pretty face and decided to write Karen and befriend her.

---

[25] Global Positioning Satellite (GPS). These ankle monitors are worn by people who are flight risks or those who need to be closely monitored by law enforcement.

With just a little attention from this guy and a few friendly letters, she was hooked. This con artist found his way into her heart. Incredibly, she fell in love with this man. I was later to find out his name. I contacted the police department here and a detective told me that he was not only a gang member, but actually a gang leader. This man had a long rap sheet of crimes against society.

The insanity continued. Karen talked to the prison chaplain and arranged for him to marry her to this gang leader. After this guy was released from prison, they moved in together. We saw pictures of this guy on the Internet, and he had gang-affiliated tattoos on his face, including a massive dog-bone tattoo across his forehead! She actually married him…in prison!

Again, no one at the church or in her family realized what had happened. After the marriage, Karen began wearing turtle-neck sweaters in the dead of summer. She was covering up all the hickeys she had around her neck. She had already changed her name and continued to serve on the worship and children's ministry teams! She kept everything secret by lying to everyone around her!

Thankfully, the lies finally began to unravel. The parents came and told me the whole truth. Like Moses, my anger become hot! With all that had already happened – the divorce, the meetings, the previous relationships, the wrong selections – she was now hiding behind all of her lies?! I was dumbfounded. How could a Christian do such things? It was difficult to believe.

I finally called her phone. I got a recording. The recording proudly announced that she was "Karen Jones." Who is Karen Jones? What happened to her real last name? It was her voice. Was this really happening?

When I finally talked to her, she told me the whole story. And she liked everything that had happened to her! There was not one ounce of remorse. She was happy now! I couldn't believe it. I can only tell you that I became extremely angry. I was on fire! I was deceived, disrespected, and used at the deepest level. Terrible thoughts ran through my mind. How dare you?! I was so enraged that I wanted bad things to happen to her.

I told her parents that she was out of the church. Immediately! She was not welcomed back. I took the extreme action, according to Scripture, of turning her over to Satan. I know that some would disagree with this action, but the apostle Paul spoke about it in 1 Corinthians 5:5 and 1 Timothy 1:20. We held a service on a Wednesday night where we told the congregation what had happened, and we handed her over to the devil so that it would bring about some genuine repentance. If you think about it, she was already captive to the devil's will according to 2 Timothy 2:26, and she was firmly in his hands.

Emotionally, I was all over the map. I was torn. I always had a lot of compassion for this young lady. Why was I so angry? Why was there so much judgment in my heart against her? Was there unforgiveness? How do I console her parents? How could they possibly remain at our church after we handed their daughter over to Satan? I was profoundly stuck. At times, I felt helpless and totally ineffective as a pastor. Honestly, I was having to process an enormous amount of pain in my heart. Beyond all these feelings, the anger was eating me up!

I was not only mad at Karen; I was very upset at the gang leader husband. Should I be reaching out to this man? All that he saw from me was a lot of rejection and condemnation. I could not accept what was happening. Everything that had happened was filled with lies, deceit, secrecy, and darkness. I saw no redeeming value.

Within about two months after that Wednesday night service, we found out that Karen's husband was physically abusing her. She had bruises all over her body. Karen's dad had seen enough. In a bold move, he went to her house and removed her from there. The game was over. She was not going back.

Shortly after this, Karen's dad stopped attending our church. Within two months, the whole family left the church. After ten long years of walking with this family through many tough issues, they walked out of my life. To add salt to the wounds, they sent me a short paragraph in an email message telling me they were leaving. No good-byes. No face to face meeting. No prayers for one another. They were just gone. We gave our life to them, and they were gone in a short email.

My first reaction was anger. My second reaction was resentment. "How dare you leave like this after all that we helped you with?" Again, I was processing a lot of pain and hurt. I never felt more useless as a pastor than after I read that email. In fact, that email made me seriously reevaluate my life. I was giving my life to the church, and often times, I was neglecting my family. I thought to myself, "Why I am giving myself like this to people who don't care and they just walk out of my life at a moment's notice?" And it was this family that always told the church that we were their "family." It all meant nothing now.

They were gone, but the anger was still with me. What was I to do? I just let them go. I spent about one month praying for them every day. It took around that long to release the bitter feelings I had toward them. I forgave them and I asked the Lord to forgive me. I blessed them in the name of the Lord and I moved on with my life. I had to move on. I couldn't stay in bitterness and rage. I learned many valuable lessons. Very importantly, I learned that a pastor has to forgive people right away, or bitterness really poisons his spirit. This was difficult. I don't often mention this, but I think the whole experience really hurt my wife. She saw what happened day after day, week after week, month after month, and year after year. We both grew in grace. We were left with scars, but we're both still standing. God is good despite our circumstances.

When Your Family Turns Against You: One of the worst rebellions in the Old Testament against God and Moses occurred in Numbers Chapter 16. The apostle Jude spoke of it as "the rebellion of Korah."[26]

The story begins with these words: "Now Korah the son of Izhar, the son of Kohath, the son of Levi...rose up against Moses." Dathan, Abiram, On, and 250 men joined in the rebellion. As you trace his family line, you see that Korah was Moses' first cousin. Izhar was Amram's younger brother. Korah was from the angry line of Levi.

Immediately, an angry exchange ensues. Moses yells, "You Levites have gone too far! Now listen, you Levites! It is against the Lord that you and all your followers have banded together!" Moses demanded that they present themselves before

---

[26] See Jude 11.

him.   They yelled back twice, "We will not come!" Numbers 16:15 reads, "Then Moses became very angry."

This was not the first time that Moses had experienced family opposition. Just a few chapters earlier, his own brother and sister rose up against him and "spoke against Moses because he had married an Ethiopian woman." Basically, Moses had married a black, "Cushite" woman. The Lord came to his defense by turning Miriam so white that she wished she was black! "Miriam became leprous, as white as snow," Numbers 12:10 says.

I praise the Lord that my wife and I have not personally experienced much opposition from immediate family members, certainly not with regard to our church or the work of the ministry. I have seen disastrous things happen in local churches when blood relatives have turned against each other and caused great turmoil in their families and within God's work. Very effective ministries have come crashing down because family members could not get along. These public clashes often generate so much anger that the bleeding wounds last for years and even decades.

The very painful conflict between Dr. Charles Stanley (father) and Andy Stanley (son), two internationally known and respected pastors, reveals that even the best of us can let division and anger rule the day. It took almost twenty years before they reconciled.

Their story reminds me of the bitter war between Jacob and Esau that lasted for decades.   I praise God that they experienced a powerful reconciliation, but think of all the years of worry, stress, tension and loss of relationship...and lots of anger. Recall that Esau was making plans to kill Jacob.

What a fearful judgment came upon Korah, Dathan, and Abiram. The earth opened its mouth and swallowed them and "their wives, sons, and little children." Then fire came from the Lord in heaven and consumed the 250 men who joined the rebellion. So Moses' cousin and all of his family perished in an instant.

To make matters worse for Moses, the next day the congregation of the Israelites blamed them (Moses and Aaron) for their deaths! "You have killed the people of the Lord," they said. From the judgments that came down, these were not "people of the Lord," but "people of the devil." In the end, fourteen thousand seven hundred people died for their complaints. What must it have been like to bury that many people? Can you imagine all the graves?! What tremendous stress and tension must have come upon Moses, the spiritual leader of Israel! His own blood relatives were judged and killed by the Lord!

Bitter Disappointment and Frustration with God's People: This is a sad reality: I have met many, many Christians and pastors who are bitter and angry at the church. Unfortunately, we have all seen the hypocrisy, strife, division, fighting, and moral failures of people who name the name of the Lord Jesus. In the last few years, I have personally known Pastors who have committed adultery, gotten drunk, stolen church finances, preached heresies, embraced homosexual marriages, or quit the ministry. Here in my city, one Senior Pastor molested two teen girls in the church's youth group, and another, a pastor and Police Chaplain, murdered the husband of a woman with whom he was having an adulterous affair. This murderer was sentenced to twenty-one years in federal prison. Who wouldn't be infuriated with such stories?

On a more practical level, so many weary soldiers of Christ have endured month after month of disappointments with God's people. Born-again Christians give their word to people, or make commitments to help, but never show up. I can give you the first and last names of fifty Christians who do not give a single penny to the work of the Lord. They are God-robbers. Churches have trouble recruiting good Sunday school teachers. Some skilled musicians begin to rely more on fog machines and multi-colored lights than the power of the Holy Spirit. The list goes on and on.

Recently, I knew the pastor of a church where the bookkeeper was stealing thousands of dollars from the church finances and using the money to gamble in Las Vegas!

I talked to a man a few years ago who had been in ministry for more than thirty years. He had just quit a church where he was the associate pastor for nearly six years. "What's wrong?" I asked. "The people are not committed, they don't tithe, nor are they serious about holiness or lost souls. They are lazy, inconsistent, late for church, and complain about everything. I'm done! I just want to serve the Lord, but they don't! I quit!" He was angry and bitter.

By the time Numbers Chapter 20, rolls around, Moses had reached the end of the rope. He had endured forty years of complaining, opposition, disappointment, rebellion, and disobedience. I imagine that his nerves were raw. The NLT translation of Psalm 106:32-33 reads, "At Meribah, they angered the Lord, causing Moses serious trouble. They made Moses angry, and he spoke foolishly."

When the Israelites arrived at Kadesh, Miriam dies. Aaron dies shortly afterward in the same chapter. Moses' brother and sister are gone. They can find no water and they are complaining again. God tells Moses to "speak to the rock" and water will come out. Instead, in a moment of desperation and frustration, Moses strikes the rock twice. He yells at them, "You rebels!" This far and no more! Moses was finished.

For his angry response, Moses missed the Promised Land. He dishonored the Lord in the presence of the people. Anger will cost you much. Put another way, you will lose a lot in your life if you continue in anger.

Perhaps one of the most difficult areas to deal with as a pastor is divorce; yet, multitudes of born-again, Spirit-filled believers cannot get along and separate in nasty ways. Kids are scattered, adults are broken, and you will see lots of anger. There is so much fighting, arguing, abuse, anger, darkness, and pain. It seems like Christians are doing everything they can to get out of the marriage relationship. What about "God hates divorce?" What about "what God has joined together, let not man put asunder?" What about "whoever divorces his wife and marries another commits adultery; and whoever marries her who is divorced from her husband commits adultery?"[27] How do you tell others about faithfulness and loyalty when your past is littered with one broken relationship after another?[28] Divorce has wreaked unbelievable destruction in Christian families.

---

[27] See Malachi 2:16, Mark 10:9, and Luke 16:18.

[28] We will teach on the anger of broken relationships when we get to Jesus and what He said in Matthew 5:21-26. I will cover this thoroughly in the next chapter.

I had known this pastor for many years. His church was close to mine. However, there was a big difference – he had about two thousand people attending his services each week. He made lots of money. He had a luxury car, expensive clothes, and many speaking engagements. He was popular speaker. He had a way with words.

He also had a way with women. He began having an affair with his church secretary. She was probably twenty-five years younger than he was. One day the secrecy and lies were uncovered, and he and his adulterous girlfriend fled our city. He divorced his wife and married this new girl. He lived in a large California city for about nine months, and then he moved back to our city. He joined a large ministry dedicated to rehabilitating men. He worked behind the scenes.

Unbelievably, he started a "new" church and gave it the same name as the original two-thousand-member church. Some people knew about his adulterous past, but most of the new people were completely unaware. The church grew. The growth was such that they had to move into bigger and bigger facilities.

My wife and I received a wedding invitation from a ministry friend. She had spent months planning everything. And guess who was going to officiate the wedding? You guessed it. This same pastor would be performing the wedding ceremony in his church! To top it off, his "new" wife was the maiden of honor!

We arrived early to the ceremony and took a seat on the front row. We were excited to see our friend get married for the first time. She was dressed in a beautiful, white wedding gown.

In the middle of the ceremony, this pastor talked to this new couple about the importance of marriage. My wife and I just looked at each other with wide eyes. What would he say?

I could not believe what I was hearing when he took about fifteen minutes to talk about being faithful to your spouse. He told the congregation what a wonderful marriage he had. He stressed repeatedly how important it was to be loyal to your wife until death do us part.

I can only say this: I was ready to stand up and scream! "You bold-face hypocrite!" I said to myself. I was so angry I almost got up and left. Enduring the rest of the ceremony was torture. As soon as the ceremony was over, I told my wife, "Let's go. I can't stand one more minute in the same building with this guy."

Once again, I did not know I was capable of such anger. This man, a pastor no less, had destroyed his marriage, dishonored marriage by committing adultery, divorced his wife, and then married his new lover. He crashed the church, rebelled against the Lord, and now he's touting the virtues of faithfulness in marriage! Just looking at a picture of this guy made me mad.

To make matters worse, the couple that was married that day began physically fighting each other within three weeks of the wedding ceremony. Within three months, they were separated. I counseled both of them. Within one year, they were divorced. Within another year, she was remarried to another man! Boy, I was ticked off! I was not very far from yelling, "You rebels!"

I told this story to give you this warning: *Watch your spirit! You will become angry at many things. In these last days, you and I will see astonishing things – injustice, murder, perversion, wickedness, genocide, corruption, wrath, deceit, rebellion, and lies on a worldwide scale.* Paul said in 2 Timothy 3:1, "In the last days, perilous (dangerous) times will come." Then he takes about six verses to describe all the unsavory characters and their evil actions that will dominate the last days.

Don't give full vent to your anger. Don't let anger master you like it mastered Cain. Guard your heart. Evil will appear to triumph in every part of our daily lives.

Get on your knees and pray. Worship God in the Spirit and in truth. Meditate on the Word of the Lord. Don't let your eyes see every evil thing happening in this world. Some of you need to turn off the TV and turn on the worship of God. Some of you need to stop feeding your spirit with all the negative news coming from ten different news sources.

And don't let your heart become bitter against the church! Is there a lot of corruption? Yes. Is there a lot of hypocrisy? Yes. Are there false believers among the true? Yes. Do pastors fail? Absolutely. But don't let these things define everything you believe about Christians and the true church. Jesus loves the church. He died for her. He promised that the gates of hell would not prevail against the church. Despite what we see and what makes us angry, we are still called to live holy and godly lives. As much as it depends on you, live for God! Don't give way to divorce, ungodliness, wickedness, and lies, but also, don't give way to anger. Stay focused on Jesus and His kingdom.

Responding to Moses & His Anger

Okay, I'm running out of room in this chapter; and yet, there is so much more to talk about regarding Moses and his anger. He was angry with Aaron's sons, Eleazar and Ithamar, in Leviticus Chapter 10. He was angry with the army officers in Numbers Chapter 31, because they did not kill all the women who had seduced Israel through the evil counsel of Balaam.

Let's give some practical advice and lessons learned from this great leader of Israel. Despite all of his failings in anger, Moses was a man called by God, and the Lord did extraordinary miracles through him that have never been repeated. He spoke with God "face to face" (Numbers 12:7-8) and he received the very words of God (the Law) (Acts 7:38).

First, I think every pastor and church leader should study his life carefully. He pastored a very large "church." Despite the large numbers of people, his real-life situations are the same ones we're facing today. I strongly believe that many, many pastors are struggling with anger issues. Pastors are under incredible stress and tension that often brings out the worst in them. I have seen angry pastors hurt many people in meetings and sermons. Too much is at stake in people's lives.

Second, where do you start when dealing with generational anger in your personal lives? What if you were raised by an angry father or mother? What if your whole family right now is filled with a bunch of hotheads?! What's the answer?

Whatever you do, don't feel sorry for yourself. Don't throw pity parties. Quit blaming everyone else for your problems. Take responsibility for your own actions and live for the Lord.

One truth that really helped me as a Christian believer was knowing that I have a new Father; I'm adopted in a new family; and I have a new DNA. I am a child of God and He loves me. I seek to model my life after my Father in heaven, not my father on earth. The Bible tells us, "Be merciful, just as your Father is merciful," "be perfect, just as your Father in heaven is perfect," and "be imitators of God as dear children." I don't feel sorry for you. You have a new family line that is not filled with anger and violent rage.

I am fully convinced of this truth in my mind: The works of the flesh are no match for the power of the Holy Spirit. In Romans and Galatians, the apostle Paul lays out the truth that Christians live by love, not by law; by the Spirit, not by the flesh; by the blessing of Abraham, not the curse of Moses (works of the law). Anger is a work of the flesh, and if we are in the flesh, we cannot please the Lord.

Were you raised by an angry father? Renounce that anger in the name of the Lord. Renounce it in the name of Jesus Christ. There is true power in the name of the Lord to "break every chain" and set the captives free. You will know the truth and the truth will set you free, and he whom the Son sets free is free indeed.

Here's a big issue for many Christians – if you have problems with anger, don't deny it! This is amazing – some of the angriest Christians I know are ones that say they don't have any problems with anger! It's so subtle. For many people, it has become so much a part of their personalities, that they can't "see it." They do almost everything with an angry spirit.

Along the same lines, just an awareness of how often we respond in anger is a huge step to being delivered from it. Do you realize how often you respond in anger? Just yesterday, I was waiting in my car for a person. They were late and it was going to make me late. I started getting angry right there in the car. I reminded myself that I was doing a series on anger and that anger is a choice. I took a few deep breaths, stopped everything, and told the Lord to help me, and then I went outside and nicely told the man to hurry because we were going to be late. The person apologized, jumped in my car, and we made it on time to the event. I suddenly realized how often I react in anger when people are late. I caught myself. Pray to the Lord for discernment.

I cannot emphasize enough how important it is to spend time with the Lord each morning, before your day gets going, and talk to Him about your temper. Pray for the Holy Spirit to restrain you. Pray that God's peace – the peace that only He can give – will flood your soul. Pray that you will not react to every difficult situation with frustration and anger. Remind yourself each morning that anger resides in the bosom of fools and that a hot-tempered man will abound in sins and transgressions. May the Lord deliver us each morning from an angry spirit.

Finally, this sounds simple, but it's hard to do – "Don't let the sun go down while you are still angry." This is so important. So many men and women let anger go on week after week, month after month, and year after year. Release people! Forgive them! Pray a blessing over those who have despitefully used you. Bless; don't curse. Come to agreement "quickly" with your adversary lest the devil take advantage of you as Jesus said in Matthew Chapter 5. When you hold on to anger, the person you are angry with binds himself to you. You will have him in your thoughts minute by minute of every day. It is a terrible bondage.

Let's pray: *"Father, in the name of Jesus Christ, I come against anger in my life. I reject anger. I renounce anger. I refuse to live with an angry spirit day by day. Deliver me, Lord, from angry outbursts that hurt my family, my friends, and my co-workers. Holy Spirit, comfort me and calm down my spirit. I have a hot temper that can only be cooled by your grace and power. Open my spiritual eyes to see all the times that I respond in anger. Break the old habits that I learned from my forefathers. Break the chains and curses of anger that have been in my family line for many generations. I pray that the angry spirit that was in my father, grandfather, and great-grandfather will have no hold on my life. I'm in a new family. I have a new DNA. I am a new creation in Christ Jesus. You are my Father in heaven and I will be like you on the earth. Thank you for delivering me from anger. In Jesus' name, Amen!"*

In the next chapter, we will carefully examine what is perhaps the greatest teaching on anger in the entire Bible. Let's look at the powerful words of the Lord Jesus Himself. So much anger is the result of broken relationships.

YouTube Videos:
- **The Christian and Anger 02a**
- **The Christian and Anger 02b**

3

Jesus & Anger

*"But I say to you that whoever is angry with his
brother without a cause shall be in danger of the
judgment. And whoever says to his brother, 'Raca'
shall be in danger of the council. But whoever says,
'You fool!' shall be in danger of hell fire."*
(Matthew 5:22)

Proverbs 15:1 is one of the most powerful and practical verses in the Bible on how to deal with anger. It says simply, "A soft (gentle) answer turns away wrath (anger), but a harsh word stirs up anger." This verse has perplexed me for years. It's not that I don't understand what it means. That's simple enough – If an angry person starts raising his voice at you, respond with a gentle answer and it will calm him down. If you use "harsh words," you will make matters far worse, and an angry exchange will ensue. My problem is why don't I obey this verse more often? I know it's there. I know it works. However, in the heat of the moment, when I'm dealing with an angry situation or person, I answer with harsh words. This is so disappointing and upsetting. Why is it that I remember the verse after the angry altercation? Why am I so easily angered? Why do

I react with aggressive words when faced with tense and difficult circumstances?

I believe the Lord has graciously helped me understand my predicament in recent years. I believe many of us have an "angry spirit." There are things in our heart that keep us on edge. We are touchy. We are easily angered. We are *not* "slow to anger." Our tempers flare quickly.

In this teaching, I want to look at perhaps the most powerful instruction on anger in the Bible. What Jesus said about anger in the Sermon on the Mount is so deep and profound, that no born-again Christian can afford to ignore it. Jesus deals with the root cause of so much anger. He doesn't just lop off the top of the weed, only to see it grow right back. He really deals with the anger issue. He pulls up the poisonous roots of anger. When we obey what Jesus said in Matthew 5:21-26, we will strike a deathblow to the angry spirit that controls so many of us.

In the Sermon on the Mount, Jesus deals with many practical things – prayer, money, anxiety, fasting, giving, love, marriage, divorce, adultery, oaths, and judging. It is very interesting to me that the very first issue the Lord addresses when it comes to relating to other people is anger. Jesus made anger an issue of righteousness that will determine if you "enter the kingdom of heaven" or not. He tells you right away that if anger escalates in your life, it could lead to "the fires of hell." Let us look at Matthew 5:21-26, verse by verse.

Anger & Murder (5:21)

One of the most convicting verses in the Bible is 1 John 3:15. It reads, "Whoever hates his brother is a murderer, and you know that no murderer has eternal life abiding in him." This is a profound word. The great apostle of love didn't write, "whoever stabs," "whoever shoots," "whoever kills," or "whoever strangles" his brother, but "whoever hates." Those who hate are those who do not love. *This verse reveals that it is possible to commit murder without committing the physical act. You can "murder" someone in your heart with anger and hatred.* One commentator calls it, "murder without knives."[29] Anger is murder in the heart just as lust is adultery in the heart (5:27-28). "As anger is the mother of murder, so lust is the mother of adultery."[30] John called them "murderers." In context, John cites "Cain" as the ultimate murderer. His anger mastered him and he physically murdered his brother Abel. Don't do that with your "brothers," the apostle says. Truly, "He who does not love his brother abides in death."[31]

The 6th Commandment says, "You shall not murder."[32] I recently asked a class of about thirty Christian students if any of them had physically committed the act of murder. "Have you actually killed a person in your life?" I asked. No one raised a hand. If we were evaluating our obedience to the 6th Commandment, then everyone passed with a perfect score.

I then asked the class, "How many people have you been angry with, say, in the last twenty years?" I added, "Raise your hand if you've been angry with anyone." Every hand in the room went up. Some people said that they've been angry with hundreds, maybe even a thousand people in their lifetimes! One person said he was angry within the last twenty minutes! Every one of us stood guilty before God. We've all failed with anger.

The difference between the two paragraphs above reveals the difference in interpretation between the "scribes and Pharisees" and Jesus on the 6th Commandment. They said it was the physical act of murder only; Jesus said you could commit murder by anger. It was the spirit of the law that really mattered. "You shall not murder" is correct. Jesus did not come to change the commandment. What was wrong was "you have *heard that it was said...*" They heard wrong. They were taught wrong. Stott pinpoints the fundamental problem: "His quarrel was not over the law, for both the Jewish leaders and Jesus accepted its divine

---

[29] *The Sermon on the Mount*, Sinclair B. Ferguson, The Banner of Truth Trust, page 82.

[30] *Ancient Commentary on Scripture, Matthew 1-13*, Volume 1a, Edited by Manlio Simonetti, InterVarsity Press, Downers Grove, Illinois, page 108. See the comments of Chromatius.

[31] See 1 John 3:12-14 and Genesis 4:6-7.

[32] See Exodus 20:13 and Deuteronomy 5:17.

authority, but over its true interpretation."[33] Carson says, "He does not begin these contrasts (5:21-48) by telling them what the Old Testament said, but *what they had heard it said*. This is an important observation, because Jesus is not negating something from the Old Testament, but something from their *understanding of it*."[34] Thus, "the contrast is not between the law given through Moses and the teaching of the Lord Jesus Christ; it is a contrast, rather, between the false interpretation of the law of Moses, and the true presentation of the law given by our Lord Himself."[35]

Notice the parallel between verses 21 and 22: "Whoever *murders* will be in danger of the judgment" and "whoever is *angry* with his brother shall be in danger of the judgment." The physical act of murder and the spiritual act of anger (in the heart) both lead to God's judgment. "Jesus did not say that anger leads to murder; He said that anger *is* murder."[36] The scribes and Pharisees had restricted the command so that anger was not a serious problem.

Anger & Danger (5:22)

It is fitting that the English word "danger" has the word "anger" in it. Anger is dangerous. I also like the catchy saying, "Anger is one letter short of danger."

Here in Matthew 5:21-26, where Jesus deals with anger, He mentions the word "danger" four times in two verses. Notice what it says, "In *danger* of the judgment" (verse 21), "in *danger* of the judgment," "in *danger* of the council," and "in *danger* of the hell fire" (verse 22).[37] Anger comes with lots of danger.

---

[33] *The Message of the Sermon on the Mount*, John R. W. Stott, The Bible Speaks Today Series, InterVarsity Press, Downers Grove, Illinois, page 77.

[34] *Jesus' Sermon on the Mount*, An Exposition of Matthew 5-10, D. A. Carson, Baker Books, Grand Rapids, Michigan, page 42.

[35] *Studies in the Sermon on the Mount*, D. Martyn Lloyd-Jones, Eerdmans Publishing, Grand Rapids, Michigan, page 194.

[36] *Be Loyal (Matthew): Following the King of Kings*, Warren W. Wiersbe, Be Series Commentary. See comments on Matthew 5:22.

[37] The word "danger" appears in the NKJV and KJV translations. Other translations use the words "subject to," "guilty of," or "judged by."

When I was a little boy growing up in my hometown, I loved the *Operation Game* (pictured). It is a battery-operated game that tests a player's hand-eye coordination. The objective of the game is to remove fictional and humorous plastic ailments from "Sam" using a pair of metal-tipped tweezers. If you accidentally touch the metal cavity opening while trying to remove one of the objects, Sam's red nose will light up and make a buzzing sound.

I was probably six or seven years old when I got this harebrained idea to put those metal tweezers into an electrical outlet. I was just curious to see what would happen. From my ignorant and naïve perspective, I thought that electricity would flow naturally from the outlet into the game through the red wire. Boy, was I wrong!

When I placed the tweezers into the outlet, immediately, a bolt of electricity shot up my hand and forearm. For a brief second, my hand froze to those tweezers and I couldn't let go. I got very scared and I somehow knew I was in serious trouble. By the grace and mercy of God, the tweezers literally melted and it left a black stain around the outlet. My arm was in pain and partly numb for several days.

I didn't realize just how dangerous that outlet was with those tweezers. If I had used just the right metal objects, I may have electrocuted myself in my own house. Used in this way, electricity can kill. The Lord spared my life.

So it is with anger. Anger is dangerous. It can kill. It can kill relationships. It can destroy families, businesses, and churches. One translation of Proverbs 27:4 reads, "Anger is cruel and can destroy like a flood." I think anger should come with warning labels: "Danger – High Voltage." And I'm wondering whether some of us hotheads should wear a T-shirt with a warning label – "*Danger*: Christian who is easily angered. Handle with great care."

"Danger" is a good translation of Greek adjective, "enochos." It means that you will be held "liable" or "responsible" for what you've done.

Anger & Your Brother (5:22)

There is a person mentioned by Jesus in each of the verses of Matthew 5:22-24. He is "his brother" (v22), "his brother" (v22),[38] "your brother" (v23), and "your brother" (v24). By definition, a "brother" is a male sibling that has the same father and mother as another person. I have four brothers who are my siblings. However, I don't think Jesus is narrowly defining "your brother" as your blood relative for there are many people who don't even have a brother. In this context, "your brother" is anyone with whom you have a personal relationship. It could be your boss at work. It could be a Christian believer at your church. It might be your sister-in-law or your uncle. It might be one of your adult children or an ex-husband or ex-boyfriend. What about a neighbor down the street or a friend across town? This list is quite long.

Notice a critical shift in words when you get to verse 25. "Your brother" becomes "your adversary."[39] Verse 25 uses the words "your adversary" twice. What Jesus is saying is this: *If your brother becomes your adversary, it's going to generate a lot of anger in your life. Basically, someone who was once your friend is now your enemy. This is the root cause of so much anger among Christian believers.* If a lot of broken relationships are in your past, then you will have a lot of burning anger in your future.

Think of all the people who have ex-husbands, ex-wives, ex-boyfriends, ex-girlfriends, ex-Pastors, ex-bosses, ex-in-laws, ex-this and ex-that. Think of all the fighting and strife that have occurred in churches that have led to division and fractured relationships. Think of all the marriages that have gone up in flames. People who once loved each other, had children together, shared Christmas and Thanksgiving, even served the Lord together, but now they are at odds and don't speak to each other. The roots of anger are deep here.

---

[38] "His brother" is mentioned twice in verse 22.

[39] I am aware that some commentators see two separate scenes – one at the synagogue (5:23-24) and one at the courtroom (5:25-26). However, the wording that begins verse 25 negates such a conclusion: "Agree with your adversary quickly…"

Anger's Escalation (5:22)

If there is one thing about anger that I have learned, it is this: Anger escalates.[40] It becomes greater, more serious and more intense. Anger's escalation is what Jesus addresses in Matthew 5:22. An angry person goes from "anger," to "raca," to "you fool!" It goes from "court" to "the fires of hell." No wonder Jesus tells us to "agree with your adversary quickly." Nip it in the bud. Don't let it go on day after day and week after week. Paul said in Ephesians 4:26-27, "Do not let the sun go down on your anger, nor give opportunity to the devil." In other words, take care of it that day. Don't let the sun set with anger still in your heart. If anger remains, you're giving the devil an opportunity to wreck your life.

When you are angry with someone, you're going to start talking (gossiping) about him. Twice in verse 22, Jesus uses these words, "Whoever says." Here we have anger in a man's speech. Anger always finds its expression through the tongue. Get around anyone who is angry and you will hear a lot of condemnation, criticism, and cursing. Once a person has been angered and offended, it is only natural to tear the other person down with your words. This is the true murder that Jesus brings up starting with verse 21. You don't need a gun or a knife to murder someone; you can do it every day with that little thing in your mouth. James 3:5-8 says this about our tongue: "The tongue is a small part of the body, but it makes great boasts. Consider what a great forest is set on fire by a small spark. The tongue also is a fire, a world of evil among the parts of the body. It corrupts the whole person, sets the whole course of his life on fire, and is itself set on fire by hell. No man can tame the tongue. It is a restless evil, full of deadly poison." Again, anger always finds its expression through the tongue, and the tongue can easily burn up your life. It comes with fire, hell, and poison. This is a very toxic mix.

One thing you will begin to do is start calling people names. "Raca" is an Aramaic word that means "empty or

---

[40] Again, some commentators disagree that Jesus teaches anger's escalation in verse 22, but there's a big difference between judgment by a "council" and getting thrown into "hell!" Anger escalates when we don't reconcile with others.

worthless one." It is someone who has an "empty head" or "no brains." Today we might call him "stupid" or "dumb." The NLT translates it, "You idiot." One Greek dictionary[41] uses the word, "buffoon." Worse, you could say, "You fool!" We're all familiar with the Greek word here. It is "mōros" from where we get the English word, "moron."

I remember very vividly what happened to me several years ago when I needed the services of a Certified Public Accountant (CPA). I asked several friends for a recommendation. I had used several CPAs in the past, but was not satisfied with most of them. One pastor friend strongly recommended a Christian man who was a CPA here in town. I got his phone number and called him right away.

I met this man at a local restaurant to discuss the documents I needed filed with a government agency. He was very friendly and he had served the Lord for many years. I thought to myself, if this works out, I will be using this Christian brother in the future whenever I need an accountant. He gave me a rough estimate of the price, which came out to around $200. We shook hands and I agreed to send him the necessary information by email and I would bring all the documents to his house the next day.

After taking him the documents, he worked on and off for several days on everything. He emailed questions back and forth. I provided him with additional information. Then, for me, something terrible happened.

He told me that he finished everything. I told him to email me the bill and I would pay him right away. I was so happy with the way everything went that I couldn't wait to pay him and move on with my life.

He sent me a bill of $2,400! Wow! I was totally offended and angered. Maybe it was a typo. Was it actually $240? I was further insulted when I saw that he gave me a special discount of 40% off the price and I "only" had to pay $1,440. Through an email, he confirmed that this was the correct amount.

I was livid. I'm not sure why, but I don't think I have been that angry in many years. How dare this man take advantage

---

[41] See the *Exegetical Dictionary of the New Testament* under the word, "Raka."

of me like this? I should have done the work myself. I wanted to scream! How could a Christian defraud another brother – a pastor at that – by charging him a fee more than ten times what he quoted me. I immediately told my wife, and her face turned pale, and then she was angry too.

It's safe to say that over the next few days, I was actually burning in anger. I began to try to figure out a way to get out of this payment. What could I do? I never wanted to see this man again. I was so upset that I finally decided to visit my pastor friend who recommended him in the first place, and express very openly how painful this experience was for me.

After a brief introduction, I said, "Pastor, do you know that CPA you recommended? That guy really took full advantage of me and burned me." With many other negative comments, I blasted that CPA to my friend. I could see that he was hurt that I had been hurt and he tried to calm me down. I closed my brief conversation with him by saying, "I will *never* use that man again! He is a snake!" I said those words with full force and venom in my tongue. I was hot! I was the actual snake!

To make a long story short, we settled on a total bill of just over $900. It was a very bitter pill to swallow. When I went to his house to drop off the check, I knocked on his door, handed him a check in an envelope, and turned away without saying a word. He asked as I walked away, "Is everything okay?" I didn't say anything. Total silence.

Thankfully, weeks later, I calmed down and got before the Lord and handed this burden over to Him. After I processed a lot of anger before the Lord in prayer, I finally had the courage to call him and ask him to forgive me for my anger. No, I never used him again, but I had to release myself from the bitterness that was working its way into my heart. In my negative attitude, I didn't want to reach the conclusion that all Christian businessmen or CPAs are crooked and take advantage of others. It did scare me a little that I could get angry enough to call another Christian brother, "a snake."

It is startling to hear Jesus say that people who reach the point of calling people derogatory names are in "danger of hell fire."[42] Someone once said, "The man who tells his brother that he is doomed to hell is in danger of hell himself."[43] Another says, "Calling someone a fool fits us for hell."[44] To call a brother, "mōros," is to be "heading straight for the fire of destruction," according to the Phillips' Translation.

People of God, don't easily dismiss this solemn truth – anger and lust are sins that lead to the fires of hell! This is serious indeed! Heart-murder and heart-adultery bring great condemnation and judgment. Jesus says in Matthew 5:22, 5:29, and 5:30, "You shall be in danger of hell fire," "your whole body will be cast into hell," and again, "your whole body will be cast into hell." Jesus said towards the end of this sermon that "Not everyone who says to Me, 'Lord, Lord,' shall enter the kingdom of heaven, but only he who does the will of My Father in heaven" (7:21).

Anger & Reconciliation (5:23-24)

Make no mistake about it – anger with man will definitely impact your relationship with God. One commentator is right: "Jesus is quite clear about this basic fact – we cannot be right with God until we are right with men. The breach between man and God could not be healed until the breach between man and man was healed."[45] Another author writes, "We always appear before God as those who are related, rightly or wrongly, to our fellow men. What we are before God involves how we are related to others."[46] I've noticed any time I've had a broken relationship with someone, the Lord always brings it up with me in prayer. I try to deny and dismiss what happened, but He always keeps it before me. I cannot escape.

---

[42] Literally in Greek, "The fire of Gehenna." This is equivalent to the "lake of fire" of Revelation or the "everlasting fire" prepared for the devil and his angels (Matthew 25:41).

[43] *The Gospel According to Matthew,* R. V. G. Tasker, Tyndale New Testament Commentaries, Eerdmans Publishing, page 69.

[44] See Ferguson, page 83.

[45] *The Gospel of Matthew*, Volume 1, Revised Edition, The Daily Study Bible Series, William Barclay, pages 142-143.

[46] See Ferguson, page 84.

Verses 23-24 need to be taken together. The startling truth about these verses is that Jesus is saying that being reconciled with your brother has a higher priority than the worship of God! Why? Because God will not accept your gift offered on the altar until you make it right with your brother. Notice that I didn't say it was more important; I just said that it has to be done *first*. In other words, reconciliation must happen *before* worship because you can't worship in spirit and in truth if there is anger in your brother's heart against you. Lloyd-Jones is right: "In the sight of God, there is no value whatsoever in an act of worship if we harbor a known sin."[47] In other words, your worship of God is empty and impossible if your heart is full of anger.

In these verses, the word "gift" is mentioned three times. It's a gift you are offering to God. When you "bring your gift," you cannot "offer your gift" until you reconcile with the offended brother. You must "leave your gift" at the altar and make things right with him. Also, where Jesus had previously been using the plural "you," now He switches to the singular "you." In fact, He uses the singular pronoun eight times in these two verses – "you," "your gift," "your brother," "you," "your gift," "your way," "your brother," and "your gift." Jesus is not speaking to the multitudes or the twelve disciples, but "to each individual among the disciples." It's as if Jesus is saying, "I'm talking to YOU!"

One translation starts, "So if you are about to place your gift on the altar and remember that someone is angry with you..." There is a vital truth that can be easily missed. Jerome, one of the early church fathers said, "He did not say, 'If you have anything against your brother,' but 'If your brother has anything against you,' so that a greater need for reconciliation is imposed on you. As long as we are unable to make peace with our brother, I do not know whether we may offer our gifts to God."[48] Therefore, "'that your brother has something against you' indicates that the person who is bringing the gift is the one at fault. This may be translated as 'that your brother has a grievance (complaint) against you (for

---

[47] Lloyd-Jones, page 200.
[48] *Ancient Commentary on Scripture, Matthew 1-13,* page 104.

something you did)' or 'is angry because of what you did.'"[49] Verse 22 says that you can be "angry with your brother," but the very next verse says, "your brother can be angry with you!" "Your brother has something against you" is the way Jesus said it.

This was a shocking revelation when Jesus first showed it to me. *I have always blamed others for my anger against them. From my perspective, it has always been my brother's fault. I'm the innocent victim. I'm the one who was right; he has always been wrong.* Jesus says, "No, you very well may be wrong. You are the one who needs to repent. You are the one who needs to initiate the first step toward reconciliation."

I see this truth not only in my own life, but in counseling sessions, especially with married couples. The wife will say, "He's the source of all our problems. He treats me bad. He makes me angry by what he does. He spends too much time at work. He flirts with other women. He won't be the spiritual leader of our home." Then he says, "She has a very critical spirit. She complains all the time. She provokes me to anger by her criticism. She expects me to do all the work, pay the bills, and do all the yard work. She's lazy!" They go back and forth – "She does this; he does that." It's like watching a tennis match. There is one argument after another being volleyed across the table. Both people claim to be right. Nobody humbles themselves before God and one another. The Lord asked Jonah twice, "Is it right for you to be angry?" He replied, "It is right for me to be angry, even unto death! It is better for me to die than to live!"[50] For some people, anger is all about rights.

A paraphrased version of verse 24 reads, "Abandon your offering, leave immediately, go to this friend and make things right. Then and only then, come back and work things out with God." This verse is teaching us that the best gift you can offer the Lord is to be reconciled with your brother. Chrysostom said long ago, "God desires to show how highly He values love and considers it to be the greatest sacrifice. So He does not even receive the sacrifice of worship without the sacrifice of love. To

---

[49] See *A Handbook on the Gospel of Matthew* from the United Bible Societies Handbook Series, B. M. Newman and P. C. Stine. See the commentary on Matthew 5:23.
[50] See Jonah 4:3, 4:4, and 4:9.

be reconciled to your brother is to offer sacrifice to God."[51] The Latin word, "reconciliare," literally means "to make friendly again." It means to turn an enemy into a friend. "Your brother" of verses 22-24 had become "your adversary" of verse 25. Several translations say, "Go and make peace with that person."[52] Here is the first step in being a "peacemaker" that Jesus just finished talking about in Matthew 5:9. And this is not an option or suggestion, because there are four Greek imperative verbs of command in this one verse – "leave!" "go your way!" "be reconciled!" and "offer!" Jesus is commanding that we take action. "Immediately, as soon as we are conscious of a broken relationship, we must take the initiative to mend it, to apologize for the grievance we have caused, to pay the debt we have left unpaid, to make amends."[53] Is it not tragic that after Jacob deceived and stole Esau's blessing, and Esau was burning in anger against Jacob's deceitfulness, that they did not reconcile for over twenty years? They lived in constant fear, suspense, and tension. These twin brothers – who lived together in the same womb – were separated for decades because they did not reconcile.

Anger's Prison & Heavy Cost (5:25-26)

After using the words, "his brother" or "your brother" four times, Jesus says that he has become "your adversary" (mentioned twice) in verse 25. This Greek word for "adversary" is not used very often in the New Testament, but it does appear in 1 Peter 5:8 where it reads, "...your adversary the devil." The Greek noun describes an opponent who brings a lawsuit against you and takes you to court. That's why you see "court language" in verse 25 – "judge," "court," "officer," and "prison."

You were once on friendly terms with this person, but now he is your enemy. These verses teach that you can pay your adversary now by reconciliation or pay in prison later by staying angry. "We put ourselves into a terrible prison when we refuse to be reconciled."[54] Once again, the Greek verb for "agree" or

---

[51] See the *Ancient Commentary on Scripture,* page 104.
[52] See the NCV and CEV translations.
[53] See Stott, page 86.
[54] See Wiersbe's comments on Matthew 5:25.

"settle" is in the imperative mood of command. Jesus is commanding us to make it right. In fact, He says to do it "quickly," otherwise, you will be "delivered to the judge," who will "hand you over to the officer," and "you will be thrown into prison." Jesus also said in Luke 12:58-59, "When you go with your adversary to the magistrate, make every effort along the way to settle with him, lest he drags you to the judge, the judge delivers you to the officer, and the officer throws you into prison. I tell you, you shall not depart from there till you have paid the very last mite."

One translation of Matthew 5:26 reads, "I promise you that you will not get out until you have paid the last cent you owe." Many translations have the words "verily," "truly," or "assuredly." It is the well-known Greek word, "amēn." Jesus used "amen" often in the gospels. It means basically that you can be 100% – absolutely and positively – sure that what He says will happen. It will come to pass. He guarantees it.

Added to that "amen" is "by no means." That phrase is also found in this sermon at 5:18 and 5:20, and twenty other times in the gospels, all by Jesus Himself. The Greek words are "ou mē." They are the strongest possible expression of saying, "Never," "no way," or "impossible!" You are absolutely going to stay in prison and pay the last penny you have to your name. In other words, you are going to be reduced to nothing. It's going to cost you everything you own. *Spiritually, you will become stuck. You will not be able to move. You're going to stay in the same place spiritually, mentally, and emotionally. You will not be able to grow in the Lord because you are trapped by anger and unforgiveness.*

Jesus uses this courtroom scene to show that you are going to be punished. He doesn't define "the prison," but when you get into anger, bitterness, and unforgiveness, you will be bound up emotionally and spiritually. You will live with a lot of stress; there will be no peace in your heart; you will be robbed of joy; you might even experience times of deep depression and hopelessness; you will have a poor and inconsistent prayer life; you will lose many close friends; a door to sickness and disease may open; or you will lose the favor of God. You may become addicted to pain medication, alcohol, or even drugs. Maybe worst of all, you may become a person filled with rage and anger. The same thing you hold against others is held against you. When you are in prison, you're not going anywhere. The sad reality is that I've experienced all of these terrible consequences because of my anger.

Let's get the bigger picture of what Jesus is teaching in this section of the Sermon on the Mount. One sin leads to another. Jesus is teaching in sequential order. Anger (21-26) often leads to adultery. Adultery (27-30) often breaks up marriages and leads to divorce. Divorce (31-32) breaks marriage vows (33-36) so that people do not "perform their oaths to the Lord" (v33).

Let's get to the point of this whole teaching – *A root cause of anger is broken relationships. If you have a lot of broken relationships in your past, you will have a lot of anger in your future. Every broken relationship causes a lot of anger.* The way of escape is to reconcile, forgive, and make peace.

As a final word for this section on anger, I want to tell you that the first step in the reconciliation process is to forgive your brother from your heart. Forgive! Release! Let him go! Do not hold on to unforgiveness for what he or she did to you.

The words, "I tell you the truth, you will not get out until you have paid the last penny," are very frightening. If you don't reconcile, and you stay in anger, and your brother stays in anger with you, it's going to cost you everything. *Nothing will be left when anger is done with you.* Interestingly, this language is found in only one other place in the gospel of Matthew. We find it in the parable of the unmerciful servant.

The story of Matthew 18:21-35 is well known. Peter asked Jesus in verse 21, "Lord, how often shall *my brother* sin against me, and I forgive him? Up to seven times?" Jesus said, "No, not seven times, but seventy times seven." Jesus then tells a parable of a king who had a servant who owed him "ten thousand talents." Because the servant could not repay the debt, the king commanded that the servant, his wife, his children, and all his possessions be sold to pay back the enormous debt. When the servant begged for patience, the king had compassion on him, and forgave him the entire debt and released him.

However, this servant had a servant that only owed him "a hundred denarii." (If ten thousand talents are equal to

$1,000,000, then a hundred denarii are $1.69.) When the servant couldn't pay, this forgiven servant angrily laid hold of this man, grabbed him by the throat, and demanded, "Pay me what you owe me!" When he couldn't, the forgiven man "threw him into prison until he could pay the debt."

When the king found out what this servant did, he was angry. Then Jesus gives us this powerful conclusion: "Should you not also have had compassion on your fellow servant, just as I had pity on you? And his master was angry, and *delivered him to the torturers until he should pay all that was owed to him.* So My heavenly Father also will do to you if each of you, from his heart, does not forgive *his brother* his trespasses" (verses 33-35). The forgiven servant merely threw his servant into prison; the king throws him into prison *and* he is tortured! The torture continues "until he pays everything that is owed." With astonishing boldness, Jesus says that that is the way Father God will treat you if you do not "forgive your brother." Peter starts with a question about "my brother," and Jesus ends with a statement about "his brother."

"And be kind to one another, tenderhearted, forgiving one another, even as God in Christ forgave you." "Bear with each other and forgive whatever grievances you may have against one another. Forgive as the Lord forgave you." "And whenever you stand praying, if you have *anything against anyone*, forgive him, that your Father in heaven may also forgive you your trespasses. But if you do not forgive, neither will your Father in heaven forgive your trespasses."[55]

As I have written in other teachings, follow the "Triple AAA" rule – forgive *Anything Against Anyone*. That's comprehensive. No one is exempt. Everything is included. Release your brother and release your anger.

Anger & Adultery (5:27-30)

Matthew 5:27-30 were not part of my original teaching on anger in 5:21-26; however, anger and adultery work together.

---

[55] See Ephesians 4:32; Colossians 3:13; and Mark 11:25-26.

These two "A's" are twin brothers that feed off of each other. Anger leads to adultery; adultery leads to anger.

In Matthew 5:27, Jesus said, "You have heard that it was said to those of old, 'You shall not commit adultery.'" This is a quote of Exodus 20:14. This is the 7th Commandment. When a married person has intercourse with someone other than his or her spouse, that is adultery. The law also prescribed the penalty for such an evil physical act: Leviticus 20:10, "The man who commits adultery with another man's wife, he who commits adultery with his neighbor's wife, the adulterer and the adulteress, shall surely be put to death." The scribes and Pharisees had reduced the sin of adultery to a physical act between a man and a woman in bed.

In one powerful verse, Jesus forever changed the location of adultery. It could be committed not only by the physical act in bed, but all alone within the heart and mind. This is commonly called "heart-adultery." Through fantasy and imagination, you can have sexual intercourse – and many other sexually explicit actions – with another woman all within the private confines of your thought life. The Lord recently spoke a word to me that drove me to my knees – "*Most Christians are not viewing pornography on the Internet, but many Christians are creating pornography in their minds.*" When I said this during a Sunday morning service, a groan shot across the entire congregation.

Matthew 5:28 is a devastating verse. Men and women of all ages and throughout human history have avoided its truth and danced around its profound implications. The Lord said, "But I say to you that whoever looks at a woman to lust for her has already committed adultery with her in his heart." *This verse lets me know that the biggest and most passionate sex organ in men and women is not between their legs but between their ears!* If you are defeated in your thought life – in your imaginations – you will be defeated every time by sexual sin. If you are out of control in your brain, you will be out of control in your private parts. Researchers and counselors are telling us that the area that most people are engaging in sexually is "self-sex." People don't need others – they are having sex all by themselves. Many people – men and women – are masturbating because their thought life is defiled and out of control. Jesus speaks of the sin of the "right hand" here in Matthew 5:30. I have learned that masturbation leaves us guilty, condemned, shamed, and defiled. It is not a "blessing" as many claim; it is a "curse" that comes after much perverted thinking. Masturbation is sex with yourself.

I want to highlight a critical little word in verse 28 that is the source of all our problems. It is the word, "lust." Our problem is not sex; it is lust. I know this is true – *Every act of physical adultery started with a lustful thought.* When a young man starts having physical intercourse with his girlfriend, it started in his mind with lustful thoughts. When a man commits physical adultery with another woman, I can assure you that he has been defeated in his mind for many years by adulterous thinking. His imaginations are defiled. Lust is the toxic fuel that inflames the passions of adultery. *No one commits physical adultery who has not been committing heart adultery.* The devil can wait for years. As you continue to meditate and fantasize about certain attractive women in your mind, you slowly but surely become more and more vulnerable and compromised. Before you know it, you're already down the road at your neighbor's house taking off your clothes. At that point, it's too late. You are consumed. Your guard is down because you've allowed your mind to run wild with perverted thoughts of illicit sex with other people.

And is it not interesting, that we only think of all the pleasure and fun that these thoughts bring us? We can imagine women doing all types of wild and sensual things to our bodies. We are so immersed with ourselves that we do not at all see *the devastating and shattering consequences of such perverted thinking!* The most devastating consequence is not when your wife finds out what you did, but when "your whole body gets cast into hell." Jesus said this twice here in 5:29-30. Sexual sin has eternal consequences. Twice we are told in Revelation that the "sexually immoral" have a place in the "lake of fire" (21:8, 22:15). Hebrews 13:4 says that the "marriage bed must be kept undefiled," because "fornicators and adulterers God will judge." God judges and punishes all sexual sin. Paul wrote in 1 Corinthians 6, Galatians 5, and Ephesians 5, that no fornicators (or adulterers) will inherit the kingdom of God. Your body was not for "sexual immorality, but for the Lord."

Jesus warned us in Mark 7:19-20, "What comes out of a man, that defiles a man. For from within, out of the heart of men, *proceed evil thoughts*, adulteries, fornications, and murders." The first thing that comes from the heart and defiles us is "evil thoughts." That's what leads to the "adulteries," "fornications," and "murders." Jesus adds, "All these evil things come from within and defile a man." These are not mistakes and problems, but "evil things." These evil things defile us. That is, they corrupt, contaminate, and pollute our lives.

No wonder Jesus uses such strong language like "pluck out your right eye" and "cut off your right hand." This is figurative language to tell us to deal ruthlessly with this sin. And the only way you can win is by the person, presence, and power of the Holy Spirit! He can and He will sanctify you! *Let me say this without hesitation – you can have a mind free and clear of perverted sexual thinking.* God's power is greater than your sin. I'll say it again – *God's power is greater than your sin.* Did not Paul say to the Galatians 5, "Walk in the Spirit, and you shall not fulfill the lust of the flesh?" Didn't he write, "Those who are Christ's have crucified the flesh with its passions and desires?" Did he not tell the Romans, "You do not walk according to the flesh, but according to the Spirit; you are not in the flesh but in the Spirit; if you live according to the flesh you will die, but if you by the Spirit put to death the deeds of the body, you will live" (8:1, 9, 13)? Paul declared this powerful truth in Romans 8:5 – "For those who live according to the flesh *set their minds* on the things of the flesh, but those who live according to the Spirit, the things of the Spirit." That is, you are not "carnally-minded," but "spiritually-minded." You are not victorious because you can say, "No." You are victorious because of the powerful Holy Spirit who lives in you. Amen.

I thought you were talking about anger? Correct. But anger opens the door to adultery and sexual sin. Anger is passionate and so is adultery. The same hormones and chemicals released in your body when you are angry are also released in your body when you are aroused sexually. When you get angry, you need to get on your knees and call on the Holy Spirit to comfort you. He will come to your aid. He will deliver you. He will empower you to overcome the temptation. You don't have to give in each time to the "corruption that is in the world through lust" (2 Peter 1:4).

May the Holy Spirit wash your brain of all the immoral thinking you have engaged in for years. May He sanctify and cleanse your thought life and your imaginations.

In the next chapter, let's look at how anger and sexual sin work together to destroy people's lives. This truth is clearly seen in the strongest man who ever lived – Samson. Anger and adultery go together.

YouTube Videos:
- **The Christian and Anger 03a**
- **The Christian and Anger 03b**

4

Samson & Anger

*"Burning with anger, Samson went up to his father's
house." (Judges 14:19)*

Physically, Samson was the strongest and most
powerful man who ever lived – not just in the Bible,
but also for all time. He performed such amazing
feats, that if Scripture had not recorded them, I would not believe
the stories. Today, fifty of the world's strongest men together
could not accomplish what he did single-handedly.

Samson ripped apart a lion with his bare hands. He
captured three hundred foxes and tied their tails together in pairs.
He killed 1,000 men with the jawbone of a donkey. He carried
Gaza's city gates uphill for nearly sixty miles and threw them near
Hebron! Finally, Samson knocked down two massive pillars in
Dagon's temple that killed 3,000 pagan worshippers.

Despite his incredible physical strength, Samson had a
glaring weakness. He was a man who was very angry. He was
burning in anger. In his fury and rage, he killed many men, or as
the Philistines said of him, "He was the destroyer of our land, and

the one who multiplied our dead (slain)."[56] His acts of revenge caused many to die.

As we taught in the last chapter, anger, if not dealt with, always escalates. Samson killed thirty men in Ashkelon; then he killed hundreds in a "great slaughter" in Timnah; then he killed 1,000 men at Lehi; and finally, he killed 3,000 at Gaza.[57] Truly, "he killed more at his death than he had killed in his life."

His anger led to another weakness, and everyone knows Samson for this weakness. He was a weak and vulnerable man regarding his sexuality. As a pastor once said, "Samson was a he-man with a she-problem." Most men don't realize that anger and adultery – the two "A's" – go together. They are twin brothers that live together in men and women. They fuel each other. Anger opens the door to adultery and adultery opens the door to anger. Jesus spoke of anger in Matthew 5:21-26, then followed it immediately with adultery in Matthew 5:27-30.

In this study, we want to look at Judges Chapters 13-16, and try to understand why the strongest man who ever lived was so weak.[58] Anger and adultery have killed many strong men. Let us see how anger ignites sexual passion and brings down many Christians. Let us also look at some practical instruction that can deliver us from this deadly trap.

Samson's Supernatural Birth

Samson was the twelfth and final judge in the Book of Judges. More personal details regarding his incredible life are given than anyone else in Judges. His story begins in Judges Chapter 13, with the Angel of the Lord's announcement of his upcoming birth. Israel's deliverer was on his way.

---

[56] See Judges 16:24.
[57] See Judges 14:19, 15:8, 15:15, 16:27, and 16:30. We must acknowledge that much of these killings involved God's deliverance from the hand of the Philistines.
[58] This is an oxymoron, but then again, Samson's life was such a contradiction. He fulfills Proverbs 7:26 – "For she (the adulteress) has cast down many wounded, and all who were slain by her were strong men."

Samson's nameless mother was barren and had no children. Suddenly, the Angel of the Lord appears to her and says, "You shall conceive and bear a son." The Angel gave her some critical instructions about her future son's hair and her personal diet. "No razor shall come upon his head, for the child shall be a Nazirite to God from the womb." As for her, "Drink no wine or similar drink nor eat anything unclean." Later on, Samson's dad, Manoah, also met the Angel of the Lord and confirmed Samson's calling.

His specific call was given before he was ever born. "He shall begin to deliver Israel out of the hand of the Philistines." God's deliverer did not need an army. Samson would destroy Israel's enemy by himself.

"The woman bore a son," "the child grew," "the Lord blessed him," and "the Spirit of the Lord began to move upon him." These few statements describe his entire youth. In the next chapter, he gets married.

Samson Rips Apart a Lion

In Judges Chapter 14, Samson finds and marries a Philistine wife against his parents' wishes. The Lord had other plans, however. God would use this marriage to begin His defeat of the Philistines.

While on his way to marry his nameless wife, a young lion comes against Samson. As if it is some  plaything, the Bible says, "The Spirit of the Lord came mightily upon him, and he tore the lion apart." To make sure we understand that Samson ripped apart the lion with his bare hands, we read, "Though he had nothing in his hand."

We must not discount how important this encounter was for Samson's confidence and future battles. If he could destroy a ferocious lion, what could he do with an uncircumcised Philistine? One commentator makes this key observation: "The mangled lion is meant as Yahweh's sign to Samson. It shows him what Yahweh can and will do through him. It should show him that the God who makes him able to tear up lions could also empower him to terrorize Philistines. Here is a preview of what Yahweh can do through Samson."[59]

David expressed this same truth many years later when someone told him that he was no match for Goliath. He said, "Your servant has killed both lion and bear; and this uncircumcised Philistine will be like one of them. The Lord, who delivered me from the paw of the lion and from the paw of the bear, He will deliver me from the hand of this Philistine."[60]

We must not minimize little victories now for they are indicators of how we will fare in bigger battles. If the three Hebrew children would not stand against unclean food in Daniel Chapter 1, they surely would have failed against the idolatrous threat in Daniel Chapter 3. The Lord told Jeremiah, "If racing against mere men makes you tired, how will you race against horses?"[61] If you can't run a mile, why sign up for a marathon?

Samson Catches 300 Foxes

I think that Samson's capture of three hundred foxes is one of the greatest miracles in the Bible. It is easy to read over it without much thought. Judges 15:4 says, "Samson went and caught three hundred foxes." That's it.

Although foxhunting has become controversial in recent years because of complaints from animal rights' activists, it has  been a popular sport in many Western nations. Have you seen pictures like the one shown here where many men, horses, and specially trained "scent hounds" go out and try to catch one fox? Do any of us realize how difficult it is to bring one home? Foxes are very crafty and evasive. Even with guns and traps, it is nearly impossible to catch one; and if you do capture it, they will give you a trophy for your incredible accomplishment!

---

[59] *Such a Great Salvation*, Exposition of the Book of Judges, Dale Ralph Davis, Baker Book House, Grand Rapids, Michigan, pages 172-173. Incidentally, this book is probably the best commentary on the Book of Judges available today. It's very good practically and theologically.
[60] See 1 Samuel 17:36-37.
[61] See Jeremiah 12:5.

Samson did not catch four or five foxes. That, in itself, would have been a tremendous achievement. He did not catch twenty-five. Maybe one thousand people with all the right equipment and animals could have captured this total; but think about it – Samson caught three hundred foxes with no horses, guns, bloodhounds, or traps! He did this by himself! Also, he was so enraged that he tied their tails together in pairs and lit them with torches. The man who was "burning with anger" burned some fields with fire. What he did outwardly was a reflection of what was happening inwardly.

Think of all the damage done by one hundred and fifty pairs of foxes that were on fire! They burned the "standing grain," "shocks," and "vineyards and olive groves."[62] We know from the first verse of Judges Chapter 15, that it was "in the time of wheat harvest." All of their daily food for the coming fall and winter was gone! These are the right conditions for a famine.

Why did Samson catch three hundred foxes? Because he was very angry with his wife and father-in-law. Do you remember the riddle that he told his thirty companions (groomsmen of his wedding)? He gave them seven days to solve the riddle. When they could not figure it out, they threatened Samson's wife with death if she didn't tell them. She didn't know herself so she begged him to tell her the answer to the riddle. He finally revealed it to her and she told them. Samson realized that they figured it out from his wife. He told them that they solved it by "plowing with my heifer." He called her a heifer! That will get you in real trouble with your wife!

In a moment of rage coupled with the Spirit's power, he went down to Ashkelon, killed thirty men, and took their clothing. He was so angry with his wife that he went back to live in "his father's house."

That living arrangement didn't last long. "After a while," Samson wanted to move back in with his Philistine wife. Actually, he just wanted to have sex with her.[63] However, there was a huge problem. The father-in-law thought that Samson was so mad at her that "he hated her." Because of this, the father-in-

---

[62] See Judges 15:5.
[63] This is clearly the language of Judges 15:1.

law gave Samson's wife in marriage to the best man from his wedding. He thought that Samson would never come back to her, and he didn't want her to live as a single woman in his house the rest of her days.

He took out his revenge on this father-in-law and his wife by capturing the 300 foxes and burning up the fields of the Philistines. The anger quickly escalated, however. The Philistines turned right around and took out their own revenge – they burned Samson's "wife and father-in-law with fire."

Again, the anger continues to escalate and now it is Samson's turn for revenge. He "attacks them hip and thigh with a great slaughter." What happens next is his third great physical feat. It was done during a time of great anger against the Philistines.

Samson Kills 1,000 Men

The Book of Judges reveals how small things can bring down big things. Ehud used a dagger to kill King Eglon (3:21); Shamgar used an ox-goad to kill six hundred Philistines (3:31); Jael, Heber's wife, used a tent peg to kill Sisera (4:21); and a woman's millstone crushed Abimelech's head (9:53). The Lord only needed three hundred men – Gideon's army – to defeat 135,000 enemy soldiers (7:22, 8:10). In our story, Samson killed 1,000 men with a donkey's jawbone (15:15).

I was at our church the other day thinking about "1,000 men." That's a lot of people! He didn't use an automatic  weapon or machine gun. How long would it take to kill 1,000 men with a jawbone? If he killed one person every minute, it would have taken him nearly seventeen straight hours. Apparently, Samson stacked these dead bodies in "heaps upon heaps" according to his poetic line in Judges 15:16 – "With the jawbone of a donkey, heaps upon heaps; with the jawbone of a donkey, I have slain a thousand men!"[64]

---

[64] Exodus 8:14 uses the same Hebrew word for "heaps" when the Egyptians stacked all the dead frogs "upon heaps" and the land "stank" or "reeked." Also, the Hebrew words, "donkey" (hachamowr) and "heaps" (chamowr), are conducive for poetry because they rhyme and

The only way we can create the *Incredible Hulk* or *Superman* is through computer animation. Such a person does not exist in real life. Only in movies can you find all the destruction of the Hulk. This is fiction. Samson, however, was the real deal. His feats will never be duplicated again.

Samson was not created in a laboratory.[65] Samson did not work out every morning at the local gymnasium. He was not a weight lifter or a body builder. We have no description of his physique anywhere in the biblical text. We are not told the size of his biceps nor how much he weighed. We are given a physical description (including height) of Goliath, but not of Samson. Why is this? *Because it wasn't his size that made him strong.*

It was the Holy Spirit that made Samson so powerful! Before he killed the lion, the Bible says, "The Spirit of the Lord came mightily upon him" (14:6). Before he killed the thirty men of Ashkelon, the Scriptures say, "The Spirit of the Lord came upon him mightily" (14:19). And before he killed 1,000 men, it reads, "The Spirit of the Lord came mightily upon him" (15:14). Even at an early age, "The Spirit of the Lord began to move upon him at Mahaneh Dan" (13:25). Samson was powerful only because the Spirit is powerful. His incredible acts of strength and skill were because he was "endued with power from on high."[66] The Spirit of God is mentioned in association with Samson more than all the other judges combined.[67]

Before I teach on Samson's last two incredible feats of strength, I want to dismiss any notion that he was a buffed power lifter that could bench press eight-hundred pounds. Twenty power lifters together could not do what Samson did by himself. Forever remove from your mind a Samson with bulging biceps and massive thighs. His strength came from the Lord. Despite his anger and rage, he was powerful in the Spirit. No one could ever do what he did regardless of his size and weight. We will never see another Samson again. He was not a "freak of nature;" he was a man empowered by the Holy Spirit.

---

are nearly identical. "With an ass, I piled up a mass" would be close English equivalent.

[65] Samson was a real person as Hebrews 11:32 confirms.

[66] These words were spoken by Jesus in Luke 24:49.

[67] See Judges 3:10, 6:34, and 11:29.

Samson Tears Off Gaza's City Gates

Judges Chapter 16 opens with an unholy scene. Samson goes to the desert town of Gaza and had sex with a Philistine prostitute. Apparently, this prostitute lived near "the gate of the city" because many "Gazites" surrounded the house to lay in wait at this gate. These men were waiting for "daylight," but Samson was waiting for "midnight." The people of Gaza would attack during the light; Samson would attack at night. Samson struck first.

When the clock struck midnight, Samson left the prostitute in her bed and went to the city gate. Although the  Gazites "kept quiet all night," Samson made a tremendous noise. Judges 16:3 says, "He took hold of the doors of the gate of the city and the two gateposts, pulled them up, bar and all, put them on his shoulders, and carried them all the way to the hill across from Hebron."

I never realized how amazing this miracle was until I looked at a Bible atlas. When I looked at a map, all I could do was shake my head. Gaza is in the west near the Mediterranean Sea. The area there is a flat desert. Now – hold on to your seats – Hebron is directly east of Gaza about sixty miles away! It is in a hilly part of Palestine. So, when the Bible says that he "carried the gates all the way up to the top of a hill near the city of Hebron," that is an accurate description of Samson's climb.

Friends, city gates (including the posts, bar, etc.) weigh thousands of pounds. The gates are massive in size and weight. It would be safe to say that even a good-sized truck would not be able to carry a load this heavy – certainly not uphill for sixty miles. There is also no way that twenty very strong men could carry these gates. I doubt that they could even lift these gates and associated attachments off the ground.

Meditate on this miracle for a few days: Ripping massive city gates out of the ground; hoisting these gates on your shoulders; and carrying them *uphill* for *sixty* miles. This defies all logic. Again, if this were not in the Bible, I would not believe it. We can only conclude that it was a supernatural act of God's power. No ordinary human could do such a thing. No power lifter or *Strongest Man* participant could accomplish this. The Lord really is Almighty God!

Think also what a miracle this is of God's sustaining power. No human being could hold up city gates weighing 1,000s of pounds. Surely, this amount of weight would crush any man, no matter how strong. The Lord supernaturally kept Samson's bones and frame from collapsing under such weight. Nothing is impossible with God!

At this point in the story, Samson is all over the map sexually. In verse 1, he had sex with a prostitute. In verse 4, he "fell in love with a woman in the Valley of Sorek whose name was Delilah." I don't believe it is an accident or coincidence that the name "Delilah" means "to weaken; make feeble; languish."[68] The man who could steady city gates on his shoulders for sixty miles was completely out of control sexually. How can you have sex with a harlot one day, and fall in love with Delilah the next day? This man was very impulsive. We will say more about this later on in this teaching.

Samson Pushes Down Massive Pillars

In Judges Chapter 16, Samson makes three remarkable statements to Delilah: "Then I shall become weak, and be like any other man" (16:7), "then I shall become weak, and be like any other man" (16:11), and "then I shall become weak, and be like any other man" (16:17). His physical strength had blinded him. His powerful feats had gone to his head. Perhaps the most terrible verdict against Samson's life is found in Judges 16:20 – "But he did not know that the Lord had left (departed) from him."

Samson really was "like any other man." He had accomplished many victories in his life, but morally, there were many failures. Regarding his anger and sexuality, he was very weak. Can we fully embrace the truth of these two penetrating verses from Proverbs: "He who is slow to anger is better than the mighty (powerful), and he who rules his spirit than he who takes a city" (16:32) and "whoever has no rule over his own spirit is like

---

[68] See the Brown Driver Briggs Hebrew lexicon or the Hebrew dictionary of Strong's Concordance.

a city broken down, without walls" (25:28). I can tell you someone who is stronger than Samson – he's the person who is "slow to anger." Samson was "broken down." Like a city without walls, he was vulnerable to the temptations of many women. Enemy forces easily overrun a city without walls.

Samson could kill 1,000 men, but one prostitute "killed" him. He could capture three hundred foxes, but one "fox" (Delilah) captured him. He could tear apart a lion, but one "lion," a pagan Philistine wife, tore him apart. Samson was not "slow to anger;" he could not "rule his spirit;" so he was a man "broken down, without walls." He fulfilled Proverbs 7:26, "For she (the adulteress) has cast down many wounded, and all who were slain (killed) by her were strong men." How appropriate is David's lament in 2 Samuel 1:19-27, "How the mighty have fallen!" *Yes, many mighty men and women have fallen by their anger and adultery.*

When badgered by his wife, he gave in to her and told the riddle; when badgered by Delilah, he gave in to her and told her the secret of his strength. *He had a way with women – he always gave in to them.* He gave in to his wife, and he lost his bet; he gave in to Delilah, and he lost his eyes. *How you deal with small temptations will be how you deal with big ones.* The Lord Jesus said it this way, "He who is faithful in what is least is faithful also in much; and he who is unjust in what is least is unjust also in much."[69] If you are compromising with porn now, you will compromise with adultery later. The door is wide open and you are vulnerable.

By the time Samson got to Delilah's lap, he was already very weak and defeated. There was no "*THEN* I shall become weak;" he was weak. He was just like every other man. A little pressure here and a little pressure there, and he would cave in to Delilah's demands.

Let us make this sobering point clear – Samson lost more than his hair; he lost his consecration before God. His uncut hair was what separated him unto God as a Nazirite. According to 2 Timothy 2:20-22, the only "vessel" that can be used by the Lord is one that is clean (sanctified; holy). Dishes and glasses must be

---

[69] See Luke 16:10.

washed before they can be used. So it is in God's kingdom – *without holiness, the Lord can't use you.*

Right after "the Lord departs from Samson," the next verse shows that his eyes were "bored out," he was chained with "bronze fetters," and he became "a grinder in the prison." What a picture?! The once powerful Samson is going around in circles in the enemy's prison! He was blind and confused!

Thank God, the story doesn't end there. Thank God, that his "hair grows again." Thank God that we serve the God of second chances! Without His mercy and grace, we are all dead in our trespasses and sins. Let us now go to his final act of strength and his premature death, but first a short personal story.

Several years ago, I went with my then teenage daughter to a large pastors' conference in Washington, D. C., our nation's capital. We also took extra time off to do sightseeing at many historical sites and government buildings.

At one point, we were in front of the Supreme Court building. The front entryway had eight marble columns that were about twenty-five feet high (pictured). The stairs leading up to the entry, the statues on the side and above, the ornate detail on the column tops, gave me  the sense that I was transported to a massive complex from ancient Rome.

I stood in-between two of the pillars and admired the size and solid construction. In my mind, I thought about Samson. To get a laugh out of my daughter, I put my right hand on one pillar and my left hand on another. I said, "Look, Leah, I'm Samson!" She laughed. "Oh, get over it dad!" she said.

The more I examined those pillars, the more I stood amazed at what Samson had done. He did not exert all his strength on just one pillar. He had "the lad" lead him to stand between two pillars. Having seen the size of the pillars at the Supreme Court Building, I doubt that Dagon's pillars would have come down if you tied chains around them and attached them to a large truck. Remember, these pillars were so massive that they held up 3,000 people. He was so powerful in the Lord's strength, that as he "leaned on them," they came crashing down.

I want to note two important points about what happened in "Dagon's temple." First, the phrase, "the lords of the Philistines," is mentioned seven times in Judges Chapter 16 (16:5, 16:8, 16:18 (2X), 16:23, 16:27, and 16:30). These "lords" were the top political and military leaders of the enemies of Israel. And notice that it says in verse 27, "*All* of the lords of the Philistines were there" and in verse 30, "the temple fell on the lords and all the people." Truly, Samson delivered Israel in one mighty blow. He wiped out all of the leadership of the Philistine cities. He was Israel's deliverer in God's hands.

Second, Judges 16:22 reads, "The hair of his head began to grow again after it had been shaven." I have heard many messages on "his hair grew again." In God's mercy and grace, He

gives us another chance. If you have failed morally – through some affair or one-night stand – get back up again. Yes, much trouble has come into your life, but your life is not over. God can use you again mightily if you allow Him to work a deep work of grace in your heart. Submit to whatever counsel, accountability, and oversight that is needed, but don't walk away from the Lord. In Judges 16:28, Samson calls on the Lord from the depths of a pagan temple. "O Lord God, remember me, I pray! Strengthen me, I pray, just this once, O God, that I may with one blow take vengeance on the Philistines for my two eyes!" What a heartfelt prayer! He really cried out to the Lord! And God answered that prayer. It is never too late to cry out to God. He will use you once again!

Samson "died with the Philistines." His brothers and father's household came down and took his body away for burial. Israel's powerful deliverer and judge was now dead. He had judged Israel for twenty years.[70]

Practical Wisdom on Anger & Sexuality

Let us now move away from the land of the Philistines and incredible acts of strength, and talk about people living in our

---

[70] See Judges 16:30-31.

day. We still have many angry people (especially men) who are battling anger and sexual issues.

In the Old Testament, we find the words "burning with anger" used often; in the New Testament, we find the words "burning with passion."[71] When a man is angry, his body releases many chemicals that are also released when he's aroused sexually. We don't realize that anger opens the door to sexual temptation. Our mind begins to think sexual thoughts. We are looking for "a release." It is like the proverbial teapot that needs to release some steam so that the pressure doesn't build up too much.

I remember years ago a man who asked for help for his brother. He asked, "Would you be able to counsel him? His marriage is in real trouble." "How long has he been married?" I asked. "Thirty years," he responded. "I'm not sure how I can help, but give him my number and have him call me," I said.

This man was a very nice person. He was soft spoken and had a peaceful demeanor. Initially, it appeared that all he needed was someone to talk to him. His business was under tremendous stress and financial difficulties. In order to keep his business afloat, he worked from the early morning hours until late at night. He had bills to pay and he could not let the business fail. His wife worked two part-time jobs and even helped with the administrative work of her husband's business to make ends meet. They were both under enormous pressure. Their heavy burdens were putting cracks in their marriage.

He was very frustrated and angry. In one of the counseling sessions with just him, he divulged that he had not had sex with his wife in over two years. When I asked why, he explained that it was because she was a little overweight. He said that she did not like him seeing her "this fat." She didn't think she was beautiful anymore. She didn't want him to see her like this with no clothes.

I finally told him after several counseling sessions: "You are living in a perfect storm. No sex with your wife. Lots of stress, frustration and anger. You're a workaholic. You don't have any times of rest or relaxation. You have no friends." He sat silently as I explained these things. I continued, "Sir, you don't have to

---

[71] See Judges 14:19 (NIV) and 1 Corinthians 7:9.

tell me anything. You can always go to a professional counselor. You may not know me well enough to confess the private inner world of your heart, but I can assure you from what I know about anger, sex, and men, that you are really struggling sexually. Surely you have a secret world of sex that no one knows but you." With that last comment, he put his head down.

"Pastor, I need to tell someone. I need to let it out because I can't go on anymore." He stopped to gather his thoughts. Finally, the dam broke. "I have been viewing pornography on my work computer for years. In fact, I have struggled with pornography since I was a teenager. I have been masturbating regularly when I shower and I watch sexually explicit movies at night after my wife goes to bed. I have lived in this secret world during the whole thirty years of our marriage." I continued to listen silently as I heard the truthfulness of his statements. He was humble and vulnerable. He added, "The sad part is that my wife knows nothing about this secret life that I've been living most of my life. It is a war that I have fought in my heart and mind, but I've never won. I'm all alone. I could never tell my wife because I'm afraid that she would leave me. My pride keeps me trapped in this deadly struggle."

How many marriages are in this same boat? A world of lust, immorality, pornography, masturbation, and affairs…and no one knows but the husband. He struggles alone. He makes 1,000 promises to God that he will never do it again, only to do it again next week and the week after that. He slowly settles it in his mind that he will never really be free. The man doesn't realize that all these sins are not only separating him from his Lord, but also from his wife. This is a very difficult life filled with condemnation and shame.

Years ago, I did a detailed Bible study on every verse that mentions "anger." I wrote down everyone's name who became angry in the Scriptures. To my surprise, there were fifty-eight people who became angry, *and all of them were men*. While we have all met some angry women, no doubt, many men are dominated by anger.

I want to speak to wives for just a minute. I would like to start with Proverbs 19:19. In the NIV translation it reads, "A hot-tempered man must pay the penalty; if you rescue him, you will have to do it again." The first thing I would say to you is that an angry spirit in a man is *very* difficult to break. Men can be continually corrected by God and others, and the problem persists. Be patient. Pray for wisdom. Being "slow to anger" is not learned easily by a man. Anger really does ensnare a man's soul. It can hound him all the days of his life. But don't lose hope. With God all things are possible and nothing is impossible for those who believe.

This is very critical: When a man is angry, he really needs comfort. He needs someone to treat him with gentleness and care. Unfortunately, for most women, they avoid their husbands at all costs when they are angry. When a woman does this, the husband is very vulnerable to many temptations – most of them sexual.

Christian believers have the greatest comforter of all. He is the Holy Spirit. *Men, when you are angry, run to the Holy Spirit.* Fall on your knees and ask for help. I am slowly learning that I must immediately pray to the Lord when I have been provoked to anger or I deliberately chose to be angry. There is an empty bedroom in my house where I usually go. I kneel and pray. "Holy Spirit, please comfort me. I'm aroused and angry. Calm my spirit. Give me the fruit of self-control so I don't do anything foolish." I have had powerful times with the Spirit in these moments of weakness and need. He is my Comforter!

There is another great comforter in a man's life. *The wife is also a man's comforter.* If your husband comes home and he's angry at his boss, a co-worker, or his work schedule, don't move away from him; go directly to him. Speak a gentle word to calm him down (Proverb 15:1). Listen to his hurt and pain. Give him a hug. Massage his shoulders, chest, and neck area. *Run your fingers through his hair.* He needs physical touch. I guarantee that he will calm down. He is aroused but your gentle touch will bring peace to his physical body and disturbed mind.

If he's angry at you or the kids, go to your room and start praying. Pray against that angry spirit. If you can, encourage him to get alone with the Holy Spirit and pray for calm. Have this agreement before he ever gets angry.

Whatever you do, don't leave him all by himself. The Lord said, "It is not good for a man to be alone," and this is especially true when he's angry and aroused. Your husband is going to look for something to bring a release. If you're not around to calm him down, he'll resort to a computer for pornography, masturbation in the bathroom or shower, a XXX movie on TV, or worse, he'll look for another woman to meet his sexual needs. Many, many men have had affairs when they've been angry. Once again, don't let him go off by himself.

Wife, you can be sure of this, if you live with a man who is given to anger, he has been battling a secret world of sexual immorality for many, many years. He is too proud to tell you. He does not want to admit that he is weak.

Don't condemn him. Fight for your husband. I know that you love him. Confront his anger issues in the name of the Lord. The angry beast can be defeated in the name of Jesus.

In many counseling sessions, men have told me that when they are angry, their wives avoid them. They go to sleep early just to keep away from them. Women truly don't like being around anger. It's a real turn off to them. These same men have told me that when the wife goes to bed, they go to their computer, laptop, tablet, or cell phone and look at porn. They go to the bathroom and masturbate. They go for a short drive and have sex with someone from work. Affairs abound when anger is aroused. I need to write this again – *Don't leave your husband all alone.* He is going to do something foolish. He will sin against the Lord and you. Sex relieves the tension from anger.

Wife, I hope you don't find this next statement offensive, but when your husband is angry, calm him down with kind words and physical touch, and then make love with him! I know a lady that used her body to minister to her husband. Whenever he was angry, she calmed him down and brought him into the bedroom. That calmed him down really quick! You may think this is carnal and sexist in nature, but great sex between a man and his wife is great spiritual warfare!

What are the biggest news items today in the world? It's all the people – men and women – who are doing foolish and perverted things sexually. Our world is dominated by the Babylonian harlot who has made the world "drunk with the wine of her fornication." *Would you rather have your husband in bed with you or with your neighbor's wife?* Anger and adultery are destroying 1,000s of *Christian* homes! Even in my small circle of influence, I have seen multitudes of families brought down by sexual sins aroused by anger. Don't let your Samson fall to his passions. Be strong in the Lord and His mighty power! Amen!

YouTube Videos:
- **The Christian and Anger 04a**
- **The Christian and Anger 04b**

THE CHRISTIAN & ANGER

5

Jonah & Anger

"But it displeased Jonah exceedingly, and he became angry. Then God said to Jonah, 'Is it right for you to be angry about the plant?' And he said, 'It is right for me to be angry, even to death!'" (Jonah 4:1, 9)

Many years ago, as a young Christian, I maintained an attitude that was completely contrary to the nature of Jesus Christ. One day, the Lord confronted me with this convicting question: *"Why is it when you sin, you want mercy; but when others sin, you want judgment?"* Like the Pharisees of old or the believers of Galatia, I was very legalistic, and legalistic Christians are always critical and judgmental of others. The verse that always drove me to my knees was James 2:13, "Judgment without mercy will be shown to anyone who has not been merciful. Mercy triumphs over judgment!"

I have found, without exception, that judgmental people are angry people. These people are angry with themselves and with others. They show no mercy, only judgment. Their first response to anything they disagree with is criticism, not compassion; condemnation, not kindness; and judgment, not mercy.

There was a man in the Bible who had an attitude like mine. He was Jonah the prophet. When he disobeyed God, and ended up in the belly of a large fish, he wanted mercy; but when the Ninevites disobeyed God, Jonah wanted judgment. When the Ninevites repented and turned from their evil ways, God showed them mercy. This act of kindness caused Jonah to burn with anger. He was angry enough to die!

One of the root causes of anger is a lack of mercy. Angry people want others punished. For these people, whatever injustice and injury someone else has done must be visited with wrath, judgment, and revenge. When provoked to anger, they want others to feel the pain they are feeling. The only way to convert such a person is for him to be given a revelation of the true God. As Jonah himself confessed, "You are a gracious and merciful God, slow to anger and abundant in lovingkindness." As Jesus told two angry apostles, "The Son of Man did not come to destroy men's lives, but to save them." The Lord also said, "For God did not send His Son into the world to condemn the world, but that the world through Him might be saved" and "for I did not come to judge the world but to save the world."[72] The Lord's heart for sinners is not condemnation, but salvation. The apostle was right – "We have seen and testify that the Father has sent the Son as Savior of the world."[73]

In this teaching, we will look closely at Jonah's anger. *He was burning with anger because he was lacking in mercy.* In the book of Jonah, we will see that anger is about rights. So many of us believe we have a "right to be angry." The Lord asked Jonah twice, "Is it right for you to be angry?" Because we have been shown abundant mercy, we have no right to be angry.

Let us learn about the Ninevites so we can understand better the depths of God's love for lost sinners and our enemies.

The Vicious Assyrians

The Bible reveals some very cruel people. Elisha said that Hazael would "kill their young men with the sword, dash their

---

[72] See Jonah 4:2; Luke 9:56; John 3:17; and John 12:47.
[73] See 1 John 4:14.

little children to the ground, and rip open their pregnant women;" the Babylonians "made Zedekiah watch as they slaughtered his sons, then they gouged out Zedekiah's eyes, bound him in bronze chains, and led him away to Babylon;" when King Herod "became exceedingly angry," he ordered the execution of "all male children two years and younger in Bethlehem and all its districts;" Pharaoh ordered "newborn boys to be cast alive into the Nile River" and drowned; "Simeon and Levi each took his sword and came boldly upon the city and killed all the males" and they cruelly "cut the tendons" of animals with swords to maim them; "Doeg the Edomite struck and killed eighty-five priests" of God, then "he struck with the edge of the sword, both men and women, children and nursing infants, oxen and donkeys and sheep – with the edge of the sword;" and "a certain Levite," after his "concubine" was gang-raped all night by the "Benjamites," he "took a knife" and "cut her up into twelve pieces, limb by limb, and sent her body parts throughout all the territory of Israel."[74]

But there was perhaps no one in the Bible as brutal, cruel, vicious, and barbaric as the Ninevites. One author writes, "Nineveh was great in sin, for the Assyrians were known far and wide for their violence, showing no mercy to their enemies. They impaled live victims on sharp poles, leaving them to roast to death in the desert sun; they beheaded people by the thousands and stacked their skulls up in piles by the city gates; and they even skinned people alive. They respected neither age nor sex and followed a policy of killing babies and young children so they wouldn't have to care for them."[75] Even the book of Jonah shows that Jonah had to "cry out against Nineveh; for their wickedness has come up before Me." The "king of Nineveh" told his subjects "…to turn every one from his evil way and from the violence that is in his hands" and "they turned from their evil way." They were "wicked" and "evil." They had "violence in their hands."

In his pride and arrogance, Sennacherib, the Assyrian king and military commander, defied and blasphemed the Lord

---

[74] See 2 Kings 8:12; 2 Kings 25:7 (NLT); Matthew 2:16 (known as the Massacre of the Innocents); Exodus 1:16, 1:22; Genesis 34:25-26, 49:5-7; and 1 Samuel 22:18-22. Many other examples could be cited.

[75] See the comments on Jonah 3:8 in Warren Wiersbe's commentary on the book of Jonah.

openly. In his blasphemy, he told King Hezekiah that no "gods of the nations" could deliver their people from my hand, so "how much less will your God be able to deliver you from my hand?"[76]

It is safe to say that Jonah, a Hebrew prophet, genuinely hated the Ninevites because they were the national enemies of Israel. They were cruel and murderous people who treated their enemies with brutality and savagery. Even monuments and ancient inscriptions testify to their violence and evil. The painting

shown here reveals an Assyrian gouging out an eye with a spear, and using the common "lip ring" by which they yanked at people's mouths to bring them into subjection. Other paintings show them stacking the bloody heads of victims in large heaps or beating people with metals rods while victims are on their knees crying for mercy. They were also known for cutting off the noses of captured enemies. No one can adequately explain the violence that was "in their hands," as the Ninevite king described.

When Jonah announced the impending judgment of God on the great city of Nineveh, the people and their king, "proclaimed a fast, put on sackcloth," "sat in ashes," and most importantly, "turned from their evil ways," then and only then, "God relented from the disaster that He had said He would bring upon them, and He did not do it."[77] When they turned from their evil ways, God turned from His judgment. *The Lord turned when they turned. It is still true today.*

One commentator says, "The book of Jonah is not so much concerned with giving us a history as it is with teaching us about the wideness of God's mercy and the narrowness of human judgment. Jonah announces doom, but God cancels the judgment after Nineveh's repentance. It is as if God were searching for an excuse – any excuse – to reverse all pronouncements of judgment. When human beings confess and repent, God responds in grace. So, what is overthrown, then, is not Nineveh, but God's own

---

[76] See 2 Chronicles 32:14.
[77] See Jonah 3:5-10.

decision. Or, to put it another way, Nineveh is overthrown in repentance."[78]

People of God, the greatest miracle in the book of Jonah was not a large fish swallowing a wayward prophet; no, it was God's compassion, mercy, and lovingkindness shown to 120,000 people who were evil and wicked. It is shocking, is it not, that Jonah ran from God's call to preach to the Ninevites, not because of disobedience, but because of God's goodness. As Jonah himself prayed, "Ah, Lord, was this not the reason why I fled previously to Tarshish; for I know that You are a gracious and merciful God, slow to anger and abundant in lovingkindness, One who relents from doing harm."[79]

Is this not the overwhelming testimony of Scripture? "The Lord, the Lord God, merciful and gracious, longsuffering, and abounding in goodness and truth, keeping mercy for thousands, forgiving iniquity and transgression and sin." "You are God, ready to pardon, gracious and merciful, slow to anger, abundant in kindness, and You did not forsake them." "You, O Lord, are a God full of compassion and gracious, longsuffering, and abundant in mercy and truth." "The Lord is merciful and gracious, slow to anger, and abounding in mercy. He will not always strive with us, nor will He keep His anger forever. He has not dealt with us according to our sins, nor punished us according to our iniquities. For as the heavens are high above the earth, so great is His mercy toward those who fear Him." "The Lord is gracious and full of compassion, slow to anger and great in mercy. The Lord is good to all, and His tender mercies are over all His works." "Return to the Lord your God, for He is gracious and merciful, slow to anger, and of great kindness; and He relents from doing harm."[80]

God is slow to anger; we are quick to anger; God is full of mercy; we are full of judgment; God is abundant in grace; we

---

[78] *Obadiah through Malachi*, William P. Brown, Westminster Bible Companion (WBC), Westminster John Knox Press, Louisville, Kentucky, pages 17, 26-27.

[79] See Jonah 4:2.

[80] See Exodus 34:6-7; Nehemiah 9:17; Psalm 86:15, 103:8-11, 145:8-9; and Joel 2:13.

are abundant in condemnation; God is kind; we are mean; God forgives; we harbor unforgiveness.

God's Love, Man's Wrath

Lest we forget – The elder brother denounced the prodigal son; the unforgiving servant choked his servant and demanded repayment; Simon the Pharisee despised the sinful woman; the Levite and the priest refused to help the Samaritan dying by the road; and the self-righteousness Pharisee looked down on the tax collector in the temple.[81] We learn that *people who judge are angry.*

One classic biblical example of the anger of judgmental people is the case of "James and John." Jesus gave them "the name, Boanerges, that is, 'Sons of Thunder.'"[82] The Aramaic word, "Boanerges," literally means "sons of violent rage." In fact, the root word appears in Daniel 3:13,[83] when Nebuchadnezzar flew "into a rage" and fury upon hearing that the three Hebrew children had not bowed down and worshiped his golden image.

James and John saw Jesus perform spectacular things. In one chapter alone, these two apostles were given power and authority over all demons, to cure diseases, and heal the sick. They saw Jesus fed five thousand men with five loaves and two fish. They just came down from the mountain where they saw Jesus's transfiguration and His magnificent glory. They were there when the Lord cast out the unclean spirit from a boy who foamed at the mouth. This chapter even says "they were all amazed at the majesty of God." I've learned that no number of miracles can restrain a man's anger.

Despite all that they saw, when Jesus determined to go to Jerusalem through the land of Samaria, James and John became very angry. They went ahead of Jesus to secure a place for Him to rest among the Samaritans. When these Samaritans refused to

---

[81] See Luke 15:28-30; Matthew 18:28-30; Luke 7:36-47, 10:30-32, and 18:9-14.

[82] See Mark 3:17.

[83] Recall that from Daniel 2:4 through the end of Daniel 7, the Book of Daniel was written in Aramaic.

receive Jesus and rejected Him instead, these "sons of violent rage" came back to Jesus and asked sincerely, "Lord, do You want us to command fire to come down from heaven and consume them, just as Elijah did?" Jesus was so upset by their question that He "rebuked them" and said, "You do not know what manner of spirit you are of." In other words, there was "a spirit" – a spirit of anger – that was emanating from them that they did not even realize. Anger was coming off of their countenance. Then the Lord delivers the bombshell: "For the Son of Man did not come to destroy men's lives but to save them." This is the message that all angry people need to take to heart – in this present time, Jesus is the Savior, not the Destroyer. The Samaritans were enemies, but Jesus came to save them. If we are honest with ourselves, often times, when we are angry with others, we want them hurt. We would like to see them punished. We will secretly rejoice when something bad happens to them. This helps justify why we're angry at them. How many of us are ready to call down fire like Elijah on those who have angered us? I wonder how many Christians would survive if God called down fire on us whenever we angered Him?

Dealing with My Anger

Over the last thirty-five years, I have met a lot of godly Pastors. Many of them have become my very close friends. However, two of these Pastors ended up turning away from the Lord – both in the same year – and it caused a lot of anger to come out of me.

I met one of the pastors through unusual circumstances. Every Tuesday for several years, I attended a local pastors' prayer group in our city that met at 8:00 am in one of the local churches. Anywhere from twenty to thirty pastors met to call on the name of the Lord for our city. It was an encouraging time of unity and togetherness that helped bond us despite coming from different churches and denominations.

When Bill[84] walked in, he looked very nervous. His eyes moved quickly here and there. He was very uneasy. It appeared

---

[84] This is not his real name. The story is true.

85

that he was in a state of panic. For some reason, I was immediately drawn to him and felt compassion for him.

As pastors began praying for various needs, suddenly, he said to everyone in the room: "I'm not sure why I'm here. My church does not believe in getting together like this with other pastors and churches." That statement startled everyone. Bill added, "I think that the Lord wants me to reach out to other ministers because I need help. My overseer is very overbearing and I need to break free from his iron grip." With that last comment, pastors got around him and began to pray. After the meeting was over, I noticed that he stayed to talk with some pastors who were in charge of the prayer meeting. Everyone else had already left. I waited around hoping to speak to him, but his conversation with two other pastors went long. I finally decided to leave.

I noticed when I went to the parking lot that there was only my car, Bill's car, and another car that I recognized belonged to another pastor. I pulled out a business card, wrote a note on the back of it, and ask this desperate pastor to call me. To make a long story short, this simple connection sent us on a fifteen-year journey of friendship that tremendously blessed both of us.

He told me that he was part of a church in the southeast part of our city. The shocking truth is this – his church actually believed that they were the only ones in the world who were the true believers in God! Everyone else was false. One of their distinctive doctrines – held unwaveringly by the founding pastor – was that as Christians, they were never to sin. This founder told his congregation that he had not sinned in nearly forty years! They used 1 John 3:6 and 3:9 as their proof texts: "Whoever abides in Him does not sin. Whoever sins has neither seen Him nor known Him. Whoever has been born of God does not sin, for His seed remains in him; and he cannot sin, because he has been born of God."

Obviously, I was completely flabbergasted by this man's beliefs. Fortunately for him, the founding pastor was on a long-term missionary assignment in Brazil, and Bill was left in charge of the local church in our city. Over the next several months, I showed him the error of this teaching, and I brought him into fellowship with many believers and churches that were following the Lord. Sometime later, mercifully, he broke away from this pastor in Brazil. It was a very liberating experience for him, and we ended up becoming best of friends.

Over the course of many years, we spend time together eating at restaurants, attending Christian events, and meeting for long discussions about the Bible. Our churches began to have joint services together on Wednesday nights. He preached in my pulpit and I preached in his. Our worship teams joined together for special times of praise and worship. I finally asked him to join our church board to help oversee the affairs of my local church. I sensed the goodness of the Lord in our relationship.

I can say without a doubt, that Bill was one of the most studious pastors I knew. He spent hours and hours each day studying and meditating on God's Word. He became a man greatly influenced by the grace of God as taught in the epistles of Paul. He had two great adult children and some beautiful grandchildren. He had been married to his wife for about forty years. She was a very sweet woman of God. He always carried gospel tracts in his vehicle, and he witnessed to unbelievers at every opportunity.

After thirty years in pastoral ministry, he decided to retire. He and his wife began looking for another church to attend after his local church merged with a larger church.

Then something went terribly wrong. He began to believe the teachings of universalism. He believed that everyone was going to get saved. He began writing me emails about this newfound "revelation" that he believed he had received from the Lord. Bill even told me in one email that the devil and Adolf Hitler were going to be in heaven. He taught that God was so merciful and kind, that He would never allow anyone to spend eternity in a conscious hell. I thought perhaps that his beliefs came from the heretic, Rob Bell, whose disastrous book, *Love Wins*, had influenced so many Christians.

Finally, in one of his emails, he wanted to meet me at Starbucks so he could convince me of the truthfulness of universalism. Unfortunately for him, I considered these beliefs heretical,[85] so there was no way I was going to give in to his new way of thinking.

I absolutely blasted him when I replied to one of his emails. I wrote, "This is total hogwash! This is a bunch of baloney! You have been deceived. This is utterly, totally false!"

After a few angry exchanges via email, he insisted again on meeting with me to win me over to his new doctrine. I completely refused. After he persisted in his emails, I finally told him that I could not fellowship with him anymore, and I even warned people in my church about him in case Bill tried to contact them. The apostle Paul "preached the faith that he once tried to destroy;"[86] but this pastor "destroyed the faith that he once tried to preach!"

I was burning in anger. I wrote to him to never contact me again unless he repented of his unbiblical beliefs. He persisted in his belief that if he could only meet with me, I would see the light regarding salvation for everyone.

At the time that our relationship fell apart, I was already going through many difficult and discouraging situations in the ministry. This very negative circumstance with this pastor really brought down my spirit. Excess adrenaline was flowing in my veins. I was nervous and fidgety. I was anxious. Why did this have to happen? Why did my friend turn into my enemy? Why was my Christian brother now my adversary? I was disturbed in my heart and mind. I genuinely loved him as my friend and brother, and now, it was all gone over a corrupt teaching. I had no answer for how to reconcile with a heretic. All I had were verses that told me to have nothing to do with such a man.

Despite my misgivings, the Holy Spirit again brought me to the verses that have always guided me during the most troubling of times. Whenever there is a broken relationship in my life, I have run to these words straight from the lips of Jesus. They are found in Matthew 5:44-48: "But I say to you, love your enemies, bless those who curse you, do good to those who hate you, and pray for those who spitefully use you and persecute you, that you

---

[85] Heretical teachings are beliefs that can condemn a person to hell. An example would be that Jesus is not God or that salvation is by works and not by God's grace through faith.
[86] See Galatians 1:23.

may be sons of your Father in heaven; for He makes His sun rise on the evil and on the good, and sends rain on the just and on the unjust. For if you love those who love you, what reward have you? Do not even the tax collectors do the same? And if you greet your brothers only, what do you do more than others? Do not even the tax collectors do so? Therefore, you shall be perfect, just as your Father in heaven is perfect." Even with a heretic, Father God wanted me to act "perfectly." I understand this to mean, "Walk in love," even toward an enemy.

When you don't know what to do, pray. When you don't know what to say, bless. When you don't how to act, love. Overcome evil with good. Never return evil for evil. Don't allow another man's evil to corrupt your good. I have never been able to reconcile with this man, but I have always been able to pray for him. God is greater than our sins, and He knows everything.

The second pastor was an amazing man. He had a godly wife and some amazing adult children who were all on fire for the Lord. His church was strong in the Lord, and he was definitely "contending for the faith that was once delivered to the saints."[87] He was a self-educated man and also had much schooling under his belt. He read widely and was knowledgeable about many things. I would say that he had a personal library of several thousand books. He was a bulldog for the truth and he cared deeply for families.

I started a small pastors' group that met in his church facilities. About five or six pastors got together every Monday for about two hours. We did this for about five years. This was one of the most spiritually profitable things I did week by week. I learned so much from these men. We strengthened each other greatly in the things of God. We definitely grew in the grace and knowledge of Jesus Christ.

Once again, as with the other pastor, we held joint services together. We preached in each other's pulpit. I attended seminars that he hosted; he attended ones where I taught. He sold one of my books in his church's bookstore. We even jointly held a marriage retreat up in the mountains that really blessed many

---

[87] See Jude 3.

people. We spoke openly to each other. God used him to bring much correction into my life. At times, he could come across rough, but I always knew his heart was for the Lord. He helped me shape much godly thinking about the church of Jesus Christ and the ways of the Lord.

I'll never forget what happened next. This pastor invited me to speak on a subject that I had written about extensively. I was so excited about the meeting, that I invited a young couple from our church to go to the Sunday evening service so they could meet my pastor friend.

Because of much prayer by many intercessors and people from our church, the Lord blessed the message and really anointed the delivery. I was very encouraged by the moving of the Holy Spirit among the people. The couple who attended the meeting was overwhelmed by the response of the people and the power of the Spirit through the teaching.

That night, the man and his wife were talking about what a blessed service it was. The man was so excited that he went home and looked up the church and this pastor on the Internet. What he saw on some YouTube videos troubled him. He saw this very pastor – my close friend and brother – smoking large pipes of tobacco and drinking mugs of German beers! He called me immediately to let me know what he found. I told him right away that there must be some kind of mistake. There's no way that this pastor could be doing something like that. But this man insisted that it was the same pastor and the same church that had produced the videos. I told him that I would look at the videos myself at the earliest opportunity.

What I saw shocked me! The videos showed this pastor, his adult sons, and many of the men in his church smoking tobacco using some elaborately crafted pipes. They actually had a "Holy Smoke Club" as part of their men's ministry! In other videos, he was condemning other Christians who were legalistic and rigid while he drank down large mugs of German beer. "I'm free," he confidently proclaimed. He put his face right up against the camera and defiantly stroked his beard outwardly in a haughty display of supposed liberty.

As I watched that video, and in light of what had just happened at his church, I stared at my computer screen in utter disbelief. I said out loud, "How dare you? How dare you do such a thing when I just told this young couple what a godly man you are and what a great congregation you have." I felt deceived. I was unclean. I also felt a lot of anger. I was hot! I remember pacing back and forth in my home office wondering what to do. I couldn't let this go past me without some type of response. But where could I begin? I was so shocked by what I was witnessing, that it was difficult to know what to say.

I called him the next day. I first asked him if those videos were really his productions. After he said, "yes," the conversation went downhill from there. We exchanged some angry words. He said, "I always felt that you were a legalistic person. You are like many Pharisees I know." I couldn't take what he was saying to me so I hung up on him. I don't remember ever doing that with another person. For the next week or two, I was on edge and very anxious.

And remember, this happened right after my other good pastor friend embraced the false teachings of universalism. For a moment, I thought something was wrong with me. I wondered whether this was all really happening to me.

"Lord, what do I do now?" I asked. I considered talking to some of his main leaders to find out if they really believed what this pastor was doing. I found out that he allowed the men of his church to drink beers right up to the point of getting drunk. He openly promoted this practice. He self-righteously thought that he would limit their debauchery by not letting them cross the line into drunkenness. His "holy smoke" meetings were also "drinking" parties. At one point I was paralyzed into inaction. I didn't know what to do. I came to believe I should go rescue the people from this man. He had gone over the edge.

In my anger, I was afraid that I was going to do something stupid. I knew all of the church leadership and they knew me. How could they tolerate what was happening? Would they listen to me? Would they see me as an enemy causing division and strife? Would they tolerate me saying anything against their beloved pastor? Many troubling thoughts came to my mind. I was burning in anger. I wanted to call down fire on him!

I'm not sure how, but I ended up in 1 Peter 2:22-23. Jesus left us "an example" of a life that we should follow. This is the famous *In His Steps* teaching from the Bible. It says, "Who committed no sin, nor was deceit found in His mouth; who, when He was reviled, did not revile in return; when He suffered, He did not threaten, but committed Himself to Him who judges righteously." One translation reads, "He did not retaliate when He was insulted, nor threaten revenge when He suffered. He left His case in the hands of God, who always judges fairly." The words stayed with me – "Jesus left His case in the hands of God." I was not going to solve this difficult situation by my anger. I remember what James said: "My dear brothers, take note of this: Everyone should be quick to listen, slow to speak and slow to become angry, for man's anger does not produce the righteousness of God."[88] It's been a hard lesson to learn, but my anger will never produce what is right. When you respond in anger, you will always make wrong decisions and regret the things that you say. It does not produce what is right, but what is wrong. I quickly realized that anger was leading me down some dark paths.

I have never been able to reconcile with this pastor or this church. Unfortunately, the good relationship that we had for many years was permanently broken. I have committed this whole situation into the hands of the Lord. In fact, just this morning, I found myself praying for this pastor. I forgive him. I release him in the name of the Lord. I pray that he will not cause anyone to stumble.

Jonah's Anger

The 4th Chapter of Jonah[89] is filled with intense emotion and great contradiction. In the opening verse, Jonah is angry at God. It reads, "But it displeased Jonah exceedingly, and he became angry." There is an interesting highlight here from the Hebrew text that reveals Jonah's passion. The main Hebrew word for "wickedness, evil," as found in Jonah 1:2 is "ra." "Ra" is found in both "displeasure" and "exceedingly." A literal translation of the Hebrew is, "It is evil to Jonah a great evil

---

[88] See James 1:19-20.

[89] Many years ago, I did a powerful verse by verse teaching on the book of Jonah. Search my website under "Jonah" at teacherofthebible.com.

(calamity)."[90] Stuart's translation reads, "It became evil to Jonah as a great evil."[91] Another commentator translates this first verse as, "But it was a very evil thing to Jonah, and he became angry." That was the evil thing to Jonah – God's compassion![92]

Furthermore, the Hebrew word for "displeasure" means "to break into pieces; to shatter." Jonah was so angry at what God did in sparing the Ninevites, that it really shattered his soul.

When God turned His anger off, Jonah turned his anger on. The Hebrew word for "anger" means "to be hot; to burn up." It appears four times in this chapter – verses 1, 4 and twice in 9. Jonah wanted Nineveh to "burn up," and the only one who burns up is him! In a few verses (4:8), God is also going to heat him up with a very hot east wind!

"Jonah's harsh attitude towards God and the Ninevites becomes all the more reprehensible when viewed against the events of Chapters 1 and 2." [93] "He who praised the gracious mercy of God in Chapter 2 turns around and deplores it in Chapter 4!"[94] "I have met men who would give their right arm to see what Jonah saw in Nineveh, for whom the privilege of being an instrument of awakening in the hands of God would be sweeter than life itself."[95] Jonah should have been praising God for everything the Lord was doing. "I doubt if there ever has been a story of God's dealings with men that should give more cause for rejoicing than the story of Jonah, and we should expect Jonah

---

[90] *Obadiah, Jonah, Micah*, T. Desmond Alexander (on Jonah), Inter-Varsity Press, Downers Grove, Illinois, page 126.

[91] *Hosea – Jonah,* Douglas Stuart, Word Biblical Commentary, Volume 31, Word Books Publisher, Waco, Texas, page 501.

[92] *The Twelve Minor Prophets*, George L. Robinson, Baker Book House, Grand Rapids, Michigan, page 53.

[93] See Alexander, page 126.

[94] *The Books of Joel, Obadiah, Jonah, and Micah*, Leslie C. Allen, The New International Commentary on the Old Testament, Eerdmans Publishing Company, Grand Rapids, Michigan, page 227.

[95] *Man Overboard! The Story of Jonah*, Sinclair B. Ferguson, The Banner of Truth Trust, Carlisle, Pennsylvania, page 78.

himself to be literally leaping with joy and thanksgiving."[96] Rather than rejoice at God's mercy, he burned in his anger.

We can agree with Stuart's conclusion on verse 1: "Jonah hated what God had done. It made him furious. If this is shocking, it is supposed to be so. Though Jonah hardly comes across as a hero anywhere in the book, he appears especially selfish, petty, temperamental, and even downright foolish in Chapter 4."[97]

Jonah 4:2 is probably the key to the whole book. We have already discussed it in some detail above, but suffice it to say that Jonah fled in Chapter 1, not because he was simply disobedient; he fled because of the mercy of God. The prophet did not want God's mercy poured out on his enemies. Friends, let us all learn that *without mercy, we will never be willing vessels for God.*

Depression often comes with anger. Many Christians who are angry are also depressed. When people are done expressing rage and anger, they come crashing down into the depths of despair. When Cain become very angry, God asked him, "Why has your countenance fallen?" He was depressed.

Here in Jonah 4:3, he wants God to "take my life from me." This is now the second time in this book that he wants to die (see Chapter 1). He says, "It is better for me to die than to live." He will say it again in 4:8, "It is better for me to die than to live." The truth is he "was angry even unto death" in 4:9. One translation of verse 3 reads, "Now let me die! I'd be better off dead." Jonah was so dejected and defeated by God's compassion on Nineveh, that he lost the will to live. Because the Ninevites don't die, he wants to die. He was on an emotional high of anger one minute, and the next, he was on a terrible low of depression. This vacillation would continue throughout this chapter. It is tragic to know that he would rather die than not get his own way. I have seen some men holding on to anger so tightly, that even though it is destroying their physical health, they refuse to let go. They would rather die than admit wrong or forgive. It's interesting that the word, "death," will be the last word Jonah utters in Scripture. There are many Jonah's in the world today.

---

[96] *The Minor Prophets, Volume 1, Hosea – Jonah*, James Montgomery Boice, An Expositional Commentary, Baker Books, Grand Rapids, Michigan, pages 301-302.

[97] See Stuart, page 502.

After God's question to Cain – "Why are you so angry? – I think Jonah 4:4 has the next great anger question: "Then the Lord said, 'Is it right for you to be angry?'" That is a key word, "right." Anger is all about rights. Anger is about entitlement. Because of the injury and injustice that others have inflicted on us, we feel justified in our anger. *We believe we have a right to be angry.* What really needed to change was not God's decision, but Jonah's attitude.

Jonah never answered God's question. He simply "walked out" on God. He walked out of the city and sat down on the east side of the city (4:5). Both Jonah and Cain never answered God's questions. If we stop and answer these questions in our own lives, I believe that the Lord will give us tremendous insight into the angry troubles of our heart. I believe he went there to see if God would somehow change His mind and destroy the city – "He sat under a shelter to see what would happen to the city."

God always has a divine "fix" for angry believers. God has been waiting for him. He "prepares" "a plant" (4:6), "a worm" (4:7), and "a vehement east wind" (4:8) just for Jonah! How does God deal with an angry prophet? He shows him kindness. "God's kindness leads you to repentance" (Romans 2:4). You can't overcome anger with anger.

This plant in Jonah 4:6 is called "qiqayon" in Hebrew. It sprang up supernaturally. If it was the "castor oil plant," it grew Jack-in-the-beanstalk fashion. These plants grew fast, but this was a miracle. Jonah "was very grateful for the plant." For the first time in the book, Jonah is supremely happy! The plant helped cool him off from the hot sun and his burning anger. The shade of the plant "delivered him from his misery." Perhaps without realizing it, Jonah is again thankful for God's mercy *toward him*, but he is not thankful for God's mercy toward the Ninevites. In verse 1, he was "exceedingly angry;" in verse 6, he was "exceedingly happy." The same Hebrew word appears in both verses.

The Lord has done this same thing to me many times before. I will be in a season of agitation, anger, complaining, and judgment, and the Lord will bless me when I least deserve it. It melts me. I'm convicted. I feel completely unworthy to receive anything when I'm troubled about many things.

Despite the "act of kindness" in verse 6, God has a painful corrective for Jonah in verse 7. It comes in the form of "a worm." The worm apparently attacked "the plant" by eating through the stem until it began "to wither" and no longer provide shade for Jonah's "head." This worm did not come from the devil – the text specifically says: "God prepared a worm." God sends "worms" into our lives to stop the madness of our anger. "Worms" have a way of humbling our pride.

One commentator suggests, "Jonah needed the worm so that he might start looking to God and not to the vine. Thank God for the vine. But thank God for the worm too. Though we may not realize it, He continues to protect us from ourselves by often removing our vines when He sees they are occupying the center of our attention. The very thing you may have considered your adversity – your worm – may be there from God's protecting hand."[98]

What happened in verse 8 drove Jonah over the edge. The worm showed up "as morning dawned," but later in the day, "the sun arose and God prepared a vehement east wind and the sun beat on Jonah's head, so that he grew faint. Then he wished death for himself."[99] Here he wants to die again. He was begging[100] to die. The angry prophet says, "It is better for me to die than to live." Once again, he would rather die than see God's kindness and mercy poured out on his enemies. Jonah is going to stubbornly hold on to his "right to be angry."

After the plant, worm, and hot wind, God again asks Jonah the same question: "Is it right for you to be angry about the plant?" This time Jonah answers with a hot-tempered word – "It is right for me to be angry, even to death!" As some translations have it, he was "mortally angry" or "deadly angry." In other words, Jonah was saying to the Lord, "I am completely justified in my anger. This is my right!"

---

[98] *Jonah: Meeting the God of the Second Chance*, O. S. Hawkins, Loizeaux Brothers, Neptune, New Jersey, page 115.

[99] In Hebrew, he literally wished for "his soul to die." See the commentary by Joyce Baldwin, page 587.

[100] The Hebrew word here, "sha'al," carries that meaning – to beg or plead.

In Jonah 4:1 and 4:3, he's angry at God because He delivers the Ninevites; in 4:9, he's angry at God because "his" plant is destroyed. So, whether deliverance or destruction, Jonah is angry. Others don't create your spirit; they only reveal it. Jonah was an angry man! He truly was burning up! And it was all over a plant that was here today, but gone tomorrow! We often see that nothing seems to satisfy angry people.

Jonah 4:10 and 4:11 both use the word, "pity." Jonah's "pity" in verse 10 was self-pity; God's "pity" in verse 11 is true mercy. The basic meaning of the Hebrew word, "hus," or "pity," is "to act with tears in one's eyes."[101]

Jonah is now trapped. God has clearly won the argument. If he can feel sorry for a plant, then surely God can feel sorry for over 120,000 people! One author writes, "If it was not right for the gourd (plant) how can it be right for Nineveh? How can it be right that Nineveh should be struck down? Yahweh was only doing for Nineveh what Jonah had insisted *he* had the right to do for a plant." Another says, "Jonah is filled with compassion regarding a mere plant, yet remains hard-hearted towards the entire population of a city."[102] We must ask the burning question: Does God have to ask Jonah for permission in order to extend mercy to lost people? Paul said in Romans that "God will have mercy on whom He wants to have mercy." He is sovereign. He doesn't have to ask permission from anyone.

Wiersbe makes this important observation: "It seems incredible, but Jonah brought a whole city to faith in the Lord and yet he didn't love the people he was preaching to! Jonah did the will of God, but not from his heart."

At the beginning, He saw their wickedness (1:2); but at the end, He saw their weakness (4:11). He started in anger, but ended in mercy. Limburg is right: "The Lord does not see in Nineveh only a great and wicked city. He also sees thousands of

---

[101] *Minor Prophets I*, Elizabeth Achtemeier, New International Biblical Commentary, Hendrickson Publishers, Peabody, Massachusetts, page 283.

[102] See Stuart, pages 506-507 and Alexander, page 130.

helpless people and innocent animals."[103]   Thus, "The book of Jonah may be summarized in one word: compassion."[104]

There are only two books in the Bible that end in a question (Jonah and Nahum), and both concern Nineveh. "The book ends with a question, a question that has no written answer. This is not a mistake. It ends on a question in order that each one who reads it might ask himself or herself the same question: Is God not right? Is He not great for showing mercy?"[105] "How did Jonah answer that question? We do not know. So the question remains for you to answer."[106]

In Summary

I challenge you right now to lay down your "rights." Are you burning in anger against someone? Maybe it is an ex-husband, ex-boss, a former pastor, or a best friend. Sadly, you might even be angry with God! Let go. Forgive. Release it. The truth is you need to release *yourself*! While you're at home sitting in your living room burning in anger, the person you are angry with may be at the beach enjoying time with her family. They're glad, but you're mad.

I challenge you to let go of anger, and instead, extend mercy. Show compassion. Be merciful as your Father in heaven is merciful. Blessed are the merciful, for they will be shown mercy. You're going to need mercy in the future, so you need to sow mercy in the present. I'm sure you are hurt, but what will hurt even more is to stay angry. Don't let the sun go down on your anger. It is going to give a foothold to the devil.

Let's pray: *"Father, in the name of Jesus Christ, I don't want to be a Jonah. Help me, fill me, and strengthen me to release my anger and extend mercy. Fill me with Your compassion and love for this person that I'm angry with. Deliver me from*

---

[103] *Hosea – Micah*, James Limburg, Interpretation, A Bible Commentary for Teaching and Preaching, John Knox Press, Atlanta, Georgia, page 157.

[104] See Robertson, page 53.

[105] See Boice, page 309.

[106] See Robertson, page 63.

judgment and condemnation. If I judge, I will be judged; if I condemn, I will be condemned; if I sow to the flesh, I'm going to reap destruction. I want to sow to the Spirit so that I reap eternal life!

Lord, I pray that You show my enemy the same mercy that You are showing me. I forgive them in the same way You have forgiven me. I love them just like You love me. Give me a heart of compassion, longsuffering, and kindness toward my enemies. If I only show love to those who are showing love to me, I'm no better than the hypocrites and the pagans. I am a son/daughter of the Most High God. I will love my enemies. I will be slow to anger and slow to wrath, because my anger does not produce the righteous life You desire. Thank You for this teaching from the book of Jonah. May I never forget what You did with people who were brutal, cruel, and evil. If You can love the Ninevites, I can love those who have hurt me. I ask all of these things in the strong name of Jesus Christ my Lord. Amen."

YouTube Videos:

- **The Christian and Anger 05a**
- **The Christian and Anger 05b**

THE CHRISTIAN & ANGER

6

Paul & Anger

"Be angry, and do not sin; do not let the sun go down
on your anger, nor give place to the devil."
(Ephesians 4:26-27)

Paul the apostle had an angry spirit about him. Anger controlled him before his conversion, and he struggled with anger after it. Before Christ, he was "destroying the church," "throwing believers in prison," "breathing threats and murder against the disciples," "doing terrible things to believers," "persecuting the Lord's followers to their death," "arresting and beating those who believed in Jesus," "violently opposing and hounding them," and "whipping them in synagogues to try to get them to curse Christ."[107] He was enraged against the church of Jesus Christ. Paul himself summed it up well when he wrote in 1 Timothy 1:13 – "I was once a blasphemer and a persecutor and a violent man." He told the Galatians, "I intensely persecuted the church of God and tried to destroy it."[108]

---

[107] Read what the Book of Acts says about "Saul of Tarsus" and Paul's personal testimony to various people – Acts 8:3, 9:1-2, 9:13-14, 9:21, 22:4-5, 22:19-20, and 26:9-11.
[108] See Galatians 1:13.

After Christ, Galatian believers angered him by their legalism and foolish behavior. He rebuked Peter to his face, and Barnabas and "the rest of the Jews" who "played the hypocrite with Peter." He got into such an argument and disagreement with Barnabas over John Mark that they separated from each other and never worked together again. My favorite was when Paul yelled at "the high priest Ananias" and said, "God will strike you, you whitewashed wall!"[109]

Make no mistake about it – God used his fiery spirit to handle many difficult situations. He wanted Judaizers mutilated in circumcision, enemies repaid for their evil deeds, and evil people handed over to Satan. He called Elymas "a child of the devil." He severely rebuked Corinthian believers who got drunk at communion services, sued each other before secular courts, abused spiritual gifts, denied the resurrection, and caused division and strife. He was mad when he found out that one person was having sex with his father's wife! When believers were led astray, he was "burning with anger."[110] Many people provoked him to wrath and anger.

Paul also wrote a lot about anger. He showed the Galatians that it was a work of the flesh. He reminded Colossian believers that anger was part of the "old man and his deeds." He taught the Ephesians to deal with anger immediately or it gives place to the devil and grieves the Holy Spirit. Let's work our way through Galatians, Colossians, and Ephesians, and learn how to overcome anger.

Galatians & Anger

The Book of Galatians is an extremely powerful book. Paul teaches Christians that we live by love, not by law; by faith in Jesus, not by works of the law; by the blessing of Abraham, not by the curse of Moses. My life is one of freedom, not of bondage;

---

[109] For all the references in this paragraph, see Galatians 1:6-8, 3:1, 2:11-14; Acts 15:36-40 and 23:3.
[110] For the references in this paragraph, see Galatians 5:12; 2 Timothy 4:14; 1 Timothy 1:20; 1 Corinthians 5:5; Acts 13:10; 1 Corinthians 11:21-22, 6:1-8, 14:23, 15:12, 1:11-13, 5:1-2; and 2 Corinthians 11:29.

I am a son, not a slave; I boast in the cross, not in the world; I'm like Isaac who inherited everything, not like Ishmael who inherited nothing; my city is the New Jerusalem which is above, not the Old Jerusalem which is here below. However, these words can just be catchy phrases on a piece of paper. How can these truths become realities in my daily life? Paul's answer is very simple – *The Holy Spirit.*

Without the Holy Spirit, the flesh will dominate your life. Starting with Chapter 3 of Galatians, when Paul teaches them how live the Christian life and not a legalistic one, he mentions the Holy Spirit by name sixteen times. How does a Christian live a strong, overcoming life? How do you dominate the flesh? Here is Paul's response: "Walk in the Spirit" (5:16), "be led by the Spirit" (5:18), "the fruit of the Spirit" (5:22), "live in the Spirit" (5:25), "walk in the Spirit" (5:25), and "sow to the Spirit" (6:8). God did not give us a program; He gave us a Person. He did not give us elaborate procedures; He gave us the power of God!

Paul taught these same truths in Romans Chapter 8. He tells us who the Spirit is: "Spirit of Christ" (8:9), "Spirit of God" (8:9, 8:14), "Spirit of life" (8:2), and "Spirit of adoption" (8:15). We're also taught about the "things of the Spirit" (8:5), "law of the Spirit" (8:2), "mind of the Spirit" (8:27), "firstfruits of the Spirit" (8:23), and the "groanings of the Spirit" (8:26). Therefore, as Christian believers, we must be "led by the Spirit" (8:14), "live by the Spirit" (8:5, 8:13), and "walk by the Spirit" (8:1, 8:4). Ultimately, it is God's "Spirit who dwells in you" (8:11). You are God's temple. The Spirit has given us complete and total victory over the "law of sin and death" (8:1), "the flesh" (8:4), "the carnal mind" (8:7), "the deeds of the body" (8:13), "the spirit of bondage to fear" (8:15), "our corrupt bodies" (8:18-23), and our weak and inconsistent prayer life (8:26-27). Everything in the believer's life revolves around the Spirit. Without Him, we are nothing! *We are not victorious because of what we can do, but by the Spirit Who lives in us!*[111]

---

[111] This entire paragraph was taken from my teaching *No Holding Back*. It is available on my website, teacherofthebible.com.

So now, let us go to the subject at hand. How does a Christian deal with his anger? The Holy Spirit of God is our remedy! Man's anger is no match for God's power.

I never realized just how many "works of the flesh" are rooted in anger. As you look over the list given in Galatians 5:19-21, you find words like "hatred," "contentions," "disagreements," "outbursts of anger/wrath," "dissensions," and "murders." None of these fleshly manifestations is possible without anger.

I really like something that Dr. S. M. Davis said in his teachings on anger. He asks these questions: Would you allow a witch to come to your house and conduct a séance? Would you allow someone into your home to commit adultery with your husband or wife? Would you permit your good friend to bring in an idol for worship and place it in the family room? Would you let your teenage son come through the door in a drunken stupor? All of these things are "works of the flesh" – "witchcraft/sorcery," "adultery," "idolatry," and "drunkenness." You would answer these questions with a resounding, "Of course not!" Then Dr. Davis drops the bomb: *"Then why do you let anger come into your homes? It is also a work of the flesh. If these other fleshly works are forbidden, why not forbid anger?"* Great questions.

Paul was absolutely right when he wrote that "the Spirit is contrary (in conflict) with the desires of the flesh" (5:17). Everything about the "fruit of the Spirit" (5:22-23) wars against the flesh. The fruit of agape love defeats anger because "love is not easily angered."[112] The fruit of self-control restraints a man's anger because we are "not to be quickly provoked in our spirit, for anger resides in the bosom of fools."[113] The fruit of peace calms down the angry man so he will be "slow to speak and slow to anger."[114] The fruit of gentleness and kindness dispels the angry spirit because "a gentle answer turns away wrath." The fruit of longsuffering or patience helps a man endure difficult trials without angry responses and complaining.[115] Neither self-will nor self-determination will ever defeat anger. Hasn't that been our problem all along? In our pride and self-efforts, we seek to prove

---

[112] See 1 Corinthians 13:5, NIV translation.
[113] See Ecclesiastes 7:9, NIV translation.
[114] See James 1:19.
[115] See Proverbs 15:1.

that we can live righteously apart from God. We don't verbalize it, but in our hearts we are saying, "Move over, Lord, I can handle my temper. Let me show you just how strong I am." *Let us stop "boasting in men," and instead, "boast in the cross!"*[116] Who will deliver us from this "body of death?" "I thank God – only through Jesus Christ our Lord!"[117]

Years ago, I believe the Lord showed me that all of us have "persons of anger" or "places of anger." What I mean is that all of us have people and places that "easily provoke" our spirit. We are angered and agitated. We "go off" on certain people, and there are places where we give "full vent" to our anger. For some people it may be a co-worker; for others it may be a sister-in-law or your adult son or daughter. They are people who know how to push your buttons and provoke you to anger. For many men and women, the place of anger is at home. I know many men who come home and take out their frustrations on the wife and children. The minute they walk through the door, they have an angry attitude that eventually blows up in a rage.

I remember vividly when our youngest child was in elementary school (Kindergarten and 1st Grade). He had the same teacher in both grades. She was an exceptional teacher in every way. While she was a disciplinarian, she also knew how to get kids on her side. Although she was tough, she knew how to show Christian love.

It seemed like every time I would pick up my son from school, the teacher would tell me that he got into trouble that day. This really upset me. Of course, I wouldn't yell and scream at him in front of the teacher or other students, but when I got to my car and strapped him into his car seat, I unleashed a torrent of harsh and condemning words. "I didn't send you to school to cause trouble; I sent you here to get a good education! How dare you disobey your teacher! You're grounded for the rest of the week! Why are you acting so foolishly?! When we get home, you're going to get a good whipping that you'll never forget!" I hate to admit this now, but these angry speeches went on for months. My

---

[116] See 1 Corinthians 3:21, 1:29 with Galatians 6:14.
[117] See Romans 7:24-25.

angry words put an unholy fear in my son that I know scarred his soul.

One afternoon I was praying in the church sanctuary. I was waiting for 3:00 p.m. so I could pick up my child from school. I was already dreading the trip to school. "What will the teacher say today?" "How can I straighten out my son today so that he behaves better at school?" I was asking myself many questions.

In that moment of prayer and reflection, it seemed like the Holy Spirit gently told me: "Have you noticed that every time you pick up your son, you respond in anger? Your car has become the place where you explode on him and release all of your frustrations." Then I heard these words: "There is a better way. Start praying every day before you pick him up. Pray against the angry spirit that you use to try to control him. *Stop yelling and start praying.*" I can only explain that an immediate sense of relief came over me. My heart was convicted and my spiritual eyes were opened. Now I could see. My son and my car were the person and place of anger for me day by day. I was amazed that I had allowed this situation to continue for so long.

I began praying to the Lord and asking for help. I prayed for Him to restrain my anger. I also found myself praying in the car all the way to the school each afternoon. I prayed for peace and calm. I saw that my son needed more than judgment; he needed encouragement. I remembered that verse in Proverbs 18:21 that says, "Death and life are in the power of the tongue, and those who love it will eat its fruit." I was spewing out a lot of death over my child. I was also eating some bitter fruit in my relationship with him. I was not "building him up;" I was "tearing him down." The apostle Paul said that he was "given authority by the Lord for edification not for destruction."[118] Unfortunately for me, the damage was already done. It's taken years to restore and heal wounds that I inflicted on a small boy.

Perhaps the first step to victory over our angry spirit is to recognize that we actually have a problem with anger. So many Christians are living in denial. The world is full of anger.

There is no victory over anger apart from the Holy Spirit. When we are weak, He is strong. Take time alone with Him each

---

[118] See 2 Corinthians 13:10 and 10:8.

day. Only He can replace your anger with love. The law cannot curb, deter, or restrain anger; only the Holy Spirit can do that.

Colossians & Anger

The Book of Colossians is a remarkable declaration of the glory, majesty, and splendor of the Lord Jesus Christ. In Him the "fullness of the Godhead dwells bodily" and "all the treasures of wisdom and knowledge are hidden." "He is sitting at the right hand of God;" "He is the image of the invisible God;" "the firstborn of all creation;" "all things were created through Him and for Him;" and "He is before all things, and in Him all things consist." "He is the head, firstborn, and the beginning" in order "that in all things He may have the preeminence." "All things were created by Him," "in Him all the fullness dwells," and "by Him all things are reconciled to Himself."[119] As you read these amazing truths about Christ, you see the words "all," "everything," and "fullness." There is no deficiency in Christ. In short, Christ is everything for the Christian believer.

Because you have "received Christ Jesus as Lord" (2:6), then "Christ is in you" (1:27), "Christ is in all (believers)" (3:11), and "the word of Christ dwells in you" (3:16). Through God's grace and mercy, you can be "a faithful brother in Christ" (1:2), "a faithful minister of Christ" (1:7), and "a bondservant of Christ" (4:12), who speaks "the mystery of Christ" (4:3). Truly, "you are complete in Him" (2:10). Your completeness, fullness, and wholeness are in Christ alone!

In the midst of all these glorious truths about Christ Jesus, Paul talks about our death! He says it is something that has already happened. Notice these critical words: "For you died" (3:3), "you died with Christ" (2:20), and "you were buried with Him" (2:12). This "death" took place at the cross nearly 2,000 years ago. It was at the cross of Christ that "we have redemption through His blood" (1:14), "peace through the blood of His cross" (1:20), because everything against us was "taken out of the way, being nailed to the cross" (2:14).

---

[119] See Colossians 2:9, 2:3, 3:1, 1:15-17, 1:16, and 1:19-20.

However, praise God, Jesus didn't stay in the grave! He rose again! He is alive! "God raised Him from the dead" (2:12) so He is now "the firstborn from the dead" (1:18). *When He rose from the dead, you rose from the dead.* "You also were raised with Him" (2:12), "He has made you alive together with Him" (2:13), and "you were raised with Christ" (3:1). "Christ is our life" (3:4) and "our life is hidden with Christ in God" (3:3). You have a powerful new life in Jesus Christ!

In summary, because you are in Christ, when Christ died, you died; when He was buried, you were buried; when He rose from the grave, you rose to newness of life! This is your complete identification with Christ at His cross and resurrection.

You might be asking yourself – Why all this talk about my death and resurrection? What does this have to do with anger? These are good questions. As you study Colossians Chapter 3 carefully, you will see how the Lord has struck a deathblow to your anger by the cross and resurrection of Christ. Let me explain.

Notice these important words in Chapter 3: "Put off" (3:8), "put off" (3:9), "put on" (3:10), "put on" (3:12), and "put on" (3:14). He teaches us to "put off anger, wrath, malice, blasphemy, lying, and filthy language." These fleshly works are part of the "old man with his deeds." The old man must be "put off." We are also to "put on the new man" with his "tender mercies, kindness, humility, meekness, longsuffering, forbearance, and forgiveness." "Above all of these things," we must "put on agape love." We will see these words again when we go to Ephesians in the next section. Paul writes, "put off the old man" (4:22) and "put on the new man" (4:24). "Put away lying" (4:25) and "put away all bitterness, wrath, anger, clamor, and evil speaking" (4:31). Instead, "put on kindness, tender mercies, and forgiveness." Paul ends by commanding us to "walk in love" (4:32-5:1).[120]

That's why Paul can write in Colossians that "you died" in one verse (3:3), and then say in another, "Therefore put to death your members which are on the earth" (3:5). At the cross, the old man died, and his deeds died with Him. In Romans 6:6, the

---

[120] Later on, Paul will also tell us to "put on the whole armor of God" and "put on the breastplate of righteousness" (6:11, 6:14).

apostle said it this way: "Knowing this, that our old man was crucified with Him, that the body of sin might be done away with, that we should no longer be slaves of sin."[121] Put off fornication, uncleanness, covetousness, anger, wrath, lying, filthy language, evil desires and unholy passions. Put off the old man and put on the new man. Therefore...

- Put off anger; put on love.
- Put off anger; put on kindness.
- Put off anger; put on forgiveness.
- Put off anger; put on tender mercies.
- Put off anger; put on meekness.
- Put off anger; put on humility.
- Put off anger; put on longsuffering.
- Put off anger; put on forbearance.[122]

As I conclude this brief study in Colossians, I believe the key verse in dealing with anger is 3:10. It reads, "Put on the new man who is renewed in knowledge according to the image of Him who created him." These words are very important, so let's look at them closely.

"Put on" – The Greek verb[123] means, "You yourself put it on." If you back up a few verses, you see the words "you yourselves" (3:7) and "you yourselves" (3:8). The Holy Spirit does His part; and you have to do yours. While we don't strive in the flesh and by self-effort, we must surrender willingly and crucify the flesh.

"The new man" – Some translations use "new self," "new nature," or "new person." I like the words "new nature." You have put on a completely new nature. You're no longer the same

---

[121] In Romans 13:12 and 13:14, Paul says to "put on the armor of light" and "put on the Lord Jesus Christ."

[122] "Forbearance" means patience, but its primary meaning is to refrain from taking action against someone. In this case, we're talking about anger. Drop it. Let it go.

[123] This is a Greek middle voice participle. It literally means, "You yourselves keep putting it on." Participles add an "-ing" to the ending of verbs, and it shows present, continuous action. This is not a one-time action.

person as when you were an unbeliever. You are a new creation in Christ. God's Spirit now lives in you. You have been totally changed.

"Renewed" – This is the word I want to focus on. Romans 12:2 teaches that the only way to be totally transformed is by "the renewing of your mind." You will never change old habits without going through a renewal process. Ephesians 4:23 also teaches the same thing: "Be renewed in the spirit of your mind." This verse is sandwiched in-between "putting off the old man" (v22) and "putting on the new man" (v24). You must renew your mind if you're going to put on a new nature. You must take on new attitudes and new thoughts. Your thinking has to change. 2 Corinthians 4:16 says that "your inward man is being renewed day by day." This is a daily task for the rest of your life. The minute you stop renewing, you're going to stop growing. This renewing does not come by your self-efforts but through the "renewing of the Holy Spirit" (Titus 3:5). What we learned in Galatians, we learn in Titus – only the Spirit can truly transform you.

Now notice what Colossians 3:10 says, "...renewed in knowledge according to the image of Him who created us." One translation says, "Becoming like the One who made you." Another reads, "Be renewed as you learn to know your Creator and become like Him." Finally, "You are becoming more and more like your Creator, and you will understand Him better."[124] *You know, the only one who can fix you is the One who made you.* You can always expect expert repairs if you send things back to the original manufacturer, be it a wristwatch or a luxury automobile. The creator knows how it was made and he can repair what's wrong. So it is with our God – He created you, and He can repair any damage. This is good news!

In Greek, "renewed"[125] means "keep on renewing" your heart and mind day by day. You can't rest on yesterday's Bible study or prayer meeting. Today is a new day. You must get up today and let the Spirit touch you. Not only are you seeking God; God is seeking you.

---

[124] See the NCV, NLT, and CEV translations.

[125] It is a Greek present tense participle; therefore, "keep on renewing."

How does this relate to anger? If you are a person who has been given to anger, you need to have your mind renewed. Every day, you need to talk to the Holy Spirit about your anger. Keep at it. Only the Spirit can break that angry spirit off your countenance. You've taken on a new nature. You are alive with Christ and seated in heavenly places. Don't settle for foolish living. Anger is foolish. Anger is cruel. Anger doesn't work the righteousness of God. Account yourself dead to sin but alive to God through Jesus Christ. The "angry man" died on the cross. The one who yells, who is easily angered, who controls others through anger – he died 2,000 years ago. A new man has been raised up with Christ. As you sense anger rise up in you, remember that the Spirit of God dwells in you. Don't give in to the angry spirit. Sow to the Spirit and not to the flesh.

Ephesians & Anger

Let's get right to the point: Paul said in Ephesians 4:26 that we are going to get angry, but we don't have to sin. The NIV translation says, "In your anger, do not sin." Another says, "When you are angry, don't let that anger make you sin." *You can be angry and not have to take it out on others.* One handbook on the Book of Ephesians says, "Do not permit how you feel to cause you to do wrong." How is this possible?

I think the answer is found in the quote Paul uses. "Be angry, and do not sin" is in italics and quotation marks in my Bible. This simply means Paul was quoting from the Old Testament. These words are found in Psalm 4:4 – "Be angry, and do not sin. Meditate within your heart on your bed, and be still. Selah." The NLT translation reads, "Don't sin by letting anger control you. Think about it overnight and remain silent." This is wisdom. Proverbs 29:22 reads, "An angry man stirs up dissension, and a hot-tempered one commits many sins." If you unleash your anger the moment you're provoked, you are going to sin and hurt a lot of people. Psalm 4:4 is telling us to stop, think first, and shut up! Go to the gym and work out. Take a shower. Go to your favorite restaurant and have a good dinner. Grab a magazine or newspaper, sit down, and relax. Give yourself some time. Think it through. Don't respond immediately in anger.

Above all, go pray. Sit quietly before the Lord. Let His holy presence temper your angry spirit.

By the sheer mercy and grace of God, I have slowly trained myself not to respond in anger with people at church. I have not always succeeded, but I'm getting better. I put my hand over my mouth and I go home. I need to cool off and gather my thoughts. Proverbs 15:18 says, "A hot-tempered man stirs up strife, but he who is slow to anger quiets contention." Things won't quiet down until you quiet down.

The truth of Psalm 4:4 goes together well with what Paul teaches in the rest of Ephesians 4:26: "Do not let the sun go down on your wrath (anger)." The wording here in Greek is in the imperative mood which means Paul is commanding us to do this. Release it. Don't harbor anger in your heart day after day, week after week, and month after month. Let it go. Forgive. Pray. Don't hold it.

The NCV says, "Be sure to stop being angry before the end of the day," and the CEV reads, "Don't go to bed angry." I like this last translation. "When the sun goes down," our day has ended. It's over. It's time to go get ready for sleep. Don't carry anger in your heart to bed, especially not against your husband or wife. Not only will you not sleep well because your spirit is agitated, but it will have disastrous long-term effects on your marriage.

There's another important reason to deal with anger that same day – if you don't, it gives an open door to the devil. Ephesians 4:27 says, "Nor give place to the devil." Paul again uses an imperative Greek verb to command believers not to give the devil "an opportunity" or "a chance." I believe when you stay angry day after day, you are sinning against the Lord, and the devil will take advantage of you. Satan will get into your relationships and wreak havoc. Paul had already warned the Ephesians in 2:2 that the devil is "the prince of the power of the air," and he's "the spirit who now works in the sons of disobedience." *Satan works directly in the hearts of disobedient people.* He is seeking these people and he devours them (1 Peter 5:8). Later in Ephesians, Paul says to "put on the whole armor of God, that you may be able to stand against the wiles (strategies) of the devil" (6:11). He also warned us, "Above all, take the shield of faith with which you will be able to quench all the fiery darts of the wicked one" (6:16). "Fiery" is actually a Greek verb that means "inflamed with anger or lust." No doubt, one of the main strategies of the devil is to keep people angry. The devil will get a "foothold" through anger and cause great destruction in your marriage.

There are two other very bad things that happen when you resort to anger. The first is found in Ephesians 4:29 and the second in 4:30. Corrupt language will flow out of your mouth and you will grieve the Holy Spirit of God. This is serious indeed!

When I'm angry, corrupt words come out of my mouth. In 4:29, Paul again commands believers – "Let no corrupt word proceed out of your mouth." "Corrupt" means "rotten" or "worthless" in Greek. Rather than say what is "bad," we must speak "what is good for necessary edification." This is important. Speak only what is good. Speak only what edifies others. When we do, "it will impart grace to the hearers." People are always listening to us. What are they hearing? "Impart grace," not condemnation.

I have a pastor friend that I admire. Whenever someone starts complaining or saying something negative, he always interjects a positive word. He finds the good in people. He speaks words that build up, not tear down. One thing I always say about him is that he is gracious. You cannot speak out grace to your hearers unless you are receiving grace from God. God only gives grace to the humble. I see now that my friend has humility in his heart. I wish I was like him!

When we are angry and corrupt words come out of our mouth, we are going to "grieve the Holy Spirit of God" (4:30). Some people "quench the Spirit;" others "grieve Him." The Spirit is gentle and kind, and He is sensitive to harsh, condemning words. Anger grieves the Spirit. Paul again uses a Greek imperative verb of command – Don't grieve the Spirit with your anger!

Ephesians 4:31-32 echoes what we already saw in Colossians 3:8-14. Once again, Paul uses command verbs in verses 31 and 32. "I command you to put away all bitterness, wrath, anger, clamor (yelling, loud quarreling), evil speaking, and all malice (ill will)." We are to replace them instead with obedience to God. Verse 32 reads, "Be kind to one another, tenderhearted, forgiving one another, even as God in Christ forgave you." Treat others the way God is treating you. What if God held a grudge and didn't forgive you for a few years? Psalm 130:3-4 reads, "If You, O Lord, kept a record of sins, O Lord, who could stand? But with You there is forgiveness!" Thank God for His forgiveness. 1 John 1:9 says, "If we confess our sins, He is faithful and just to forgive us our sins and cleanse us from all unrighteousness." Are you holding bitterness against someone right now? Do you have ill will toward a co-worker? Are you "speaking evil" of another Christian? Put it away from you! Go pray. Call out to the Holy Spirit to renew your thinking.

Years ago, a Christian man who was a bold witness for Christ started attending our church. He talked to everyone about Jesus. Unfortunately, he had a bad habit. After nearly every Sunday service, he called me to complain about something that took place in the service. "I don't like what he said at church." "The music was too loud." "You shouldn't allow women to speak in church." "Why didn't you rebuke that sister in public?" "How come more of our people are not standing up for righteousness?" "Our church is becoming lukewarm." After every service, I began to dread his calls. "What will he complain about now?" I asked myself. When I looked at the caller ID on my cell phone, I often just let the call go to voice mail. It was draining just to hear all of his complaints.

One day I went to the church office and saw that our answering machine had a message. Interestingly, the person who called was this man's mother! "Hello Pastor Charlie. I'm Howard's mother (not his real name). Can you please call me? I need to talk to you." She left her phone number. I wondered why she called me. I went into the church sanctuary and prayed.

I called her back. She said, "My son has left your church. Please don't worry about it. I work at a church in administration and I see everything that Pastors go through. Howard's basic problem is that he hates his father. He has been enraged against him for years. He condemns him openly on every occasion. My husband is a Christian believer, but he smokes. Howard tells him all the time that he's going to hell! No one in our family can tolerate my son. All of us are going to hell. It seems, to my son, that he's the only one going to heaven! He's very bitter and angry. He's been this way for many years. Please forgive him."

Wow! This man's anger and bitterness against his father tainted his view of everyone. I read this morning in Exodus 21, that the law put to death anyone who curses his father or mother (v17).

Are you bitter? Are you angry? Let people go! Release them! The "old you" died. That old man given to anger and wrath was put to death. You are a new man governed by the Holy Spirit and walking in love. Forgive even as Christ forgave you. Love even as Christ loved you. Reject the angry spirit! Walk in love.

YouTube Videos:
- **The Christian and Anger 06a**
- **The Christian and Anger 06b**

THE CHRISTIAN & ANGER

7

Proverbs & Anger

*"Make no friendship with an angry man, and with a
furious man do not go, lest you learn his ways and set
a snare for your soul." (Proverbs 22:24-25)*

This is now our seventh teaching on anger. By way
of review, here is a brief summary of our previous
teachings and conclusions in the first six chapters:

- *Cain & Anger*: Cain was so angry, he murdered his
  brother. We saw that anger is a choice. Many people are
  angry and stay angry because they choose to live that way.
- *Moses & Anger*: Moses was the angriest man in the Bible.
  He murdered a man at the beginning of his life, and he
  lost the Promised Land at the end – all because of anger.
  With him, we saw that anger is generational (through
  Levi) and it is learned from parents.
- *Jesus & Anger*: Jesus goes right to the heart of our anger
  issues. Anger is dangerous. Broken relationships are the
  root cause of most anger problems. Through
  reconciliation, anger is defused.
- *Samson & Anger*: Anger and sexual sin go together. Even
  though Samson was the strongest man who ever lived, he

was also one of the weakest. He could have sex with a prostitute one day, rip off Gaza's gates the next, and fall for Delilah's sexual temptations soon after. He was all over the map sexually. The two "A's" – Anger and Adultery – go together.

- *Jonah & Anger*: With Jonah, we learned that anger is about rights. "Do you have a right to be angry?" He was "angry enough to die." Even though he was shown incredible mercy by the Lord, he was not willing to show it to others. Like James and John after him, Jonah never learned that the Lord did not come "to destroy men's lives but to save them." Anger seeks to destroy. Angry people are lacking in mercy.

- *Paul & Anger*: Paul had an angry spirit about him. Before his conversion, he was enraged against the church; after his conversion, he struggled with anger. He taught us that anger is a work of the flesh, part of the "old man and his fleshly deeds," gives place to the devil, and grieves the Holy Spirit. We defeat anger by the Spirit of God and a renewed mind.

The Foolishness of Anger

Even though Proverbs and Ecclesiastes emphasize the wisdom of God, they both say a lot about fools and their foolishness. There are over one hundred verses in these two books that reveal the true nature of "fools," "foolishness," "foolish men," "foolish women," "foolish sons," "chattering fools," "a fool's lips," "a fool's mouth," "a fool's back," "a fool's wrath," "the hand of fools," "the eyes of fools," "the mouth of fools," and "the way of fools." Truly, "fools proclaim foolishness" and there is "the folly of fools" and "the foolishness of fools." That amazing 26th Chapter opens with twelve straight verses on fools, and it concludes, "As a dog returns to his own vomit, so a fool repeats his folly." Anger is a folly that a fool repeats.

Years ago, I taught a course in a Bible school on the Book of Ecclesiastes.[126] It was such a powerful class as we went through it verse by verse. Written when he was old, Solomon made piercing observations about human nature and conduct. With sharp wit and remarkable insight, he exposed the "vanity" and "futility" of human life. In Ecclesiastes 7:9, the wisest man who ever lived said this about anger: "Do not be hasty in your spirit to be angry, for anger rests in the bosom of fools." The CEV translation reads, "Only fools get angry quickly," and the NLT says, "Control your temper, for anger labels you a fool." Anger is foolish and it identifies you as a fool.

Let us now go to the book that says the most about anger – the Book of Proverbs. God's wisdom reveals its many dangers and snares. Fools are hot-tempered; the wise are "slow to anger."

Proverbs 14:17 – The Man with a Short Nose

Proverbs 14:17 – "A quick-tempered man does foolish things."

Instead of "quick-tempered," the KJV uses "soon angry" and the NLT says "short-tempered." The Hebrew word for "tempered" or "angry" means "nostrils" or "nose," and it is translated that way in many verses of the Old Testament.[127] And "soon" is a word that means "short." Literally, in Hebrew, "quick-tempered" describes a person with a "short-nose." The writer is telling us of  a person who has a short fuse. If you light a bomb with a short fuse, it could blow up in your face. He is someone that goes from calm to angry in five seconds. Such a person is very touchy. He is easily angered. It does not take very much to set him off.

This verse simply tells us that quick-tempered people will do foolish things. He will do things that are crazy, rash, reckless, and irrational. It's interesting that the verse just before this one says in the NIV, "A fool is hotheaded and reckless" (14:16).

---

[126] See the entire course that's available for free at my website, teacherofthebible.com. See under *Ecclesiastes*.

[127] For example, see Genesis 2:7; Exodus 15:8; Numbers 11:20; 2 Kings 19:28; Psalm 115:6; Isaiah 2:22; and Amos 4:10.

People do things totally out of character when they are angry. One commentator says, "His anger clouds his judgment and robs him of all sense of perspective; so he reacts and acts impetuously in ways which are out of all proportion to the situation."[128]

One day I received a phone call from a lady at our church who was very frightened. She asked if I could come over right away to her house. When I asked what was going on, she said, "I'm getting ready to move out. My husband has lost his mind due to his anger. I'm very afraid of him and I can't go back to the house without someone else present." Suddenly, I was afraid too. Did he have a gun? Had he attacked her? Should I go over with a police escort? There was a lot of uneasiness in my mind.

When I got to the house, she was waiting for me in the driveway. The husband was inside. Both of them were Christian believers and members of our church. They had been married about three months and already cracks and fractures appeared in their marriage relationship. After greeting her, I could see that she was scared. She did not want to go inside the house. I went inside first and talked to him. He was sitting on the couch staring at the wall in front of him.

He said, "I don't know everything that's going on, but I've really lost my cool. She has provoked me to anger."

"Why is she so scared? Why won't she come in the house? What have you done to her?" I asked. About this time, she quietly walked in through the front door.

What I learned was this – he had taken some expensive porcelain plates from the kitchen, and in a moment of rage, rather than throw them directly at her, he threw several of them against the wall not far from where she was sitting in the family room. They smashed into a thousand pieces. Porcelain pieces were scattered everywhere in the carpet and on the couch. These shattered pieces were a clear reflection of their marriage.

"He does this to intimidate me," she said. "This is the way he treats me to keep me under his control and make sure he gets his own way. I'm always walking on eggshells around him.

---

[128] *Proverbs*, Kenneth T. Aitken, The Daily Study Bible Series, The Westminster Press, page 108.

The slightest problem easily angers him. I can no longer live with him. I don't feel safe here."

I sat there with this husband in stunned silence. While we both looked at the ground, she walked briskly into the bedroom. From where I was sitting, I could see that she was packing her clothes in a suitcase and some bags. As far as she was concerned, it was over. Within about ten minutes, she walked silently out the door. While I did not officiate his wedding, I was there to hear the vows of "until death do us part." That meant nothing now. His angry spirit had destroyed his marriage.

Never forget: *"A quick-tempered man does foolish things."* Throwing porcelain plates just above your wife's head to intimidate her is utterly foolish. I wondered where this man had learned to do that.

Friends, there is a better way. In that great chapter on love, Paul told the Corinthians, "Love is not easily angered."[129] Agape love is "slow to anger." The fuse is very long. It is not easily provoked. I don't want to make things too simple, but where is the agape love? This husband's biggest failure was his lack of love. Colossians 3:19 says, "Husbands, love your wives and do not be harsh with them." In the original Greek language, Paul commanded, "Don't be embittered against them."[130] Christian women – no, all women – cannot handle bitter men and harsh words. Peter told us to "treat them with respect." "Gentleness" and "kindness" do not come naturally to a man. How we need the Holy Spirit to work this fruit in our lives!

It's important to see that the same Hebrew word for "angry" in verse 17 is also found in the same chapter at 14:29. It reads, "He who is slow to wrath (anger) has great understanding,

---

[129] See 1 Corinthians 13:5.

[130] See the NKJV translation. We know Paul commanded this because he used a Greek imperative verb of command. It's interesting to me that apart from this verse in Colossians, this Greek verb appears only in Revelation a few times including Revelation 8:11. There it speaks of a star named "Wormwood" that caused many waters to become "bitter," and "many men died from the water." What a picture of our relationship with our wives!

but a quick-tempered man displays folly."[131]   The NLT says, "People with understanding control their anger; a hot temper shows great foolishness." "Slow to wrath" in Hebrew is literally "long-nosed." In other words, he has a "long fuse." It's just the opposite of the "short fused" person above. James 1:19-20 say, "My beloved brethren, let everyone be swift to hear, slow to speak, slow to wrath, because the wrath (anger) of man does not work the righteousness of God." Man's anger is wrong. It cannot do right.

However, what positive truth does Proverbs 14:29 teach us? Notice what it says again: "He who is slow to wrath *has great understanding*." "Understanding" is a major theme in Proverbs. It means that we are able to grasp the meaning or perceive what's happening in our life. So many men and women don't understand their anger. They don't know why they are so angry. That's why I have written so extensively on this subject. We must learn to *hold anger back*. Pray for the Lord to give you understanding in how you relate to your spouse, children, co-workers, friends, and extended family. Tell your wife to restrain you when you're getting out of hand. Know for sure that anger is foolish. You will do stupid things. You will live in regret over what you've done and what you've said. I pray that the Holy Spirit will give me "great understanding" so that I can control my temper, see the dangers ahead, and stop before I go over the cliff! Proverbs 22:3 and 27:12 say exactly the same thing: "The prudent man sees danger and takes refuge, but the simple keep going and suffer for it."

Proverbs 15:1 – A Gentle Answer Turns Away Anger

Proverbs 15:1 – "A soft answer turns away wrath, but a harsh word stirs up anger."

In terms of practical advice, nothing in Proverbs beats the wisdom of this verse. Day by day, this is perhaps the best way to defeat anger around you. When you are in the presence of an angry person, you can calm him down with "a soft answer." You

---

[131] The first half of the verse is from the NKJV; the second half is from the NIV.

answer with "soft, gentle words." Many of us underestimate the potency of gentleness. It is a fruit of the Spirit, so it has the Spirit's power!

Proverbs 25:15 reads, "A gentle tongue breaks the bone" or "soft speech can break bones." One translation of the entire verse says, "With patience, you can make anyone change their thinking, even a ruler. Gentle speech is very powerful."[132] I used to live in the desert and found many bones of dead animals. Some of those bones were nearly impossible to break. The Bible uses this picture language to show the powerful effect of gentle words. An interesting verse in Ecclesiastes 10:4 says, "If the anger of the ruler rises against you, do not leave your place, for calmness will lay great offenses to rest." "Calmness" can turn tense and angry situations into peaceful and tranquil ones.

On April 4, 1968, James Earl Ray killed Martin Luther King Jr. in Memphis, Tennessee. The shocking murder caused an outpouring of grief and anger in the United States and throughout the world. There were riots in over one hundred U.S. cities. However, there was no rioting in one major city. That city was Chicago.

In an amazing display of the power of "soft words," Robert Kennedy, brother of John F. Kennedy, delivered a short speech that calmed down the entire city of Chicago. Here is a brief excerpt from his address:

"I'm only going to talk to you just for a minute or so this evening, because I have some – some very sad news for all of you. Could you lower those signs, please? I have some very sad news for all of you, and, I think, sad news for all of our fellow citizens, and people who  love peace all over the world; and that is that Martin Luther King was shot and was killed tonight in Memphis, Tennessee."

With that opening comment, screams and gasps rippled through the large crowd that heard him. He spoke in a low-tone with gentle words. Then he added these words:

"For those of you who are black – considering the evidence evidently is that there were white people who were

---

responsible – you can be filled with bitterness, and with hatred, and a desire for revenge. For those of you who are black and are tempted to fill with – be filled with hatred and mistrust of the injustice of such an act, against all white people, I would only say that I can also feel in my own heart the same kind of feeling. I had a member of my family killed, but he was killed by a white man."

Here was a man who understood grief at the deepest level. His own brother, the President of the United States, was brutally assassinated in Dallas, Texas only a few years before. He could empathize with the audience. It was this remarkable speech, given in a low voice, with words of compassion, that stopped a large city from rioting! The entire city of Chicago stayed calm – all because of gentle words – while the rest of the country erupted in violent rage at the assassination.

Going back to Proverbs 15:1, did you notice the words "stirs up anger." The Old English word "stirs" means "agitate." Harsh words "stir up" or "agitate" anger. It adds fuel to the fire. Proverbs says a lot about "stirring up." Consider these verses: "Hatred stirs up strife," "a wrathful (angry) man stirs up strife," "he who is of a proud heart stirs up strife," "an angry man stirs up strife," and "stirring up anger produces strife."[133] Hate, pride, and anger stir up more of the same. How we need the Lord to control our tongues! The Psalmist said, "Set a guard, O Lord, over my mouth; keep watch over the door of my lips."[134] Once we let out those angry words through "the door" of our lips, there is no retracting what was said. Proverbs 29:22 says, "An angry man stirs up strife, and a furious man abounds in transgression." Another translation reads, "An angry man stirs up dissension, and a hot-tempered one commits many sins." Angry people stir up a lot of arguments, conflicts, divisions, and fights. This is the hard truth: You are going to "commit many sins." We are going to do and say many foolish things.

Proverbs 13:3 says, "He who guards his mouth preserves his life, but he who opens wide his lips shall have destruction." "Opening wide your lips" just means "talking too much."

---

[133] See Proverbs 10:12, 15:18, 28:25, 29:22, and 30:33.
[134] See Psalm 141:3.

James 1:26 gives us these convicting words, "If you claim to be religious but don't control your tongue, you are fooling yourself and your religion is worthless."

Here in Proverbs, Chapter 15, we find another important verse on anger. Verse 18 reveals more of the same. "A wrathful (angry, hot-tempered) man stirs up strife, but he who is slow to anger allays contention." "Allays" means "to calm; to relieve." Another translation says, "A hot-tempered man stirs up dissension, but a patient man calms a quarrel." Once again, the person with the "long nose" or "slow to anger" is the one who calms down quarrels. I think Proverbs 15:1 and 15:18 say the same thing just using different words. We see all the same words again: "Anger," "stirs up," "contention," "strife," and "slow to anger." Remember Proverbs 29:8, "Mockers stir up a city, but wise men turn away anger." Another translation says, "The wise will calm anger." So many people are stirring up anger, but *wise men turn away anger*. We are seeking everything in our power to calm things down, not stir things up. Proverbs 30:33 reads, "As the beating of cream yields butter and striking the nose causes bleeding, so stirring up anger causes quarrels." Again, we can calm things down or we can stir things up. I recently told a group of Christian men from the *Teen Challenge* ministry – "Jesus called us to be peacemakers, not troublemakers." A groan went over the crowd after that statement. Too many people, including Christians, are troublemakers because they have an angry spirit.

I learned long ago that there is one virtue that all of us need – *I mean ALL of us*. We all need "patience." If you are patient, you will be "perfect," "lacking nothing." This is definitely an area where all of us lack. I lack patience; therefore, I give way to anger. Angry people are impatient people.

Proverbs 19:11 – Overlooking Insults & Offenses

This verse reads as follows: "*The discretion of a man makes him slow to anger, and his glory is to overlook a transgression.*" This verse is full of wisdom on dealing with anger.

The English word "discretion" comes from the Latin word that means "discerning." People who have tact, understanding, and common sense avoid saying harsh and embarrassing things that upset others. When James was talking about the tongue, he said, "Consider what a great forest is set on fire by a small (tiny) spark." So true! One little word, said in the wrong way, can generate so much anger. Christians with discretion use wisdom before they speak. Discretion makes us "slow to anger." Once again, it gives us a "long nose." We don't blow up right away.

Here is one of the keys to avoid a lot of anger: "Overlook a transgression." So many of us angry folks are touchy. Every little thing bothers us. We are annoyed, irritated, riled, and provoked by so many things. We don't overlook transgressions; we nurse these sins in our hearts. We detect every small offense. Nothing escapes our notice. Here is my word to you – let it go! Release the offender! Move on with your life. Why dwell on everybody's sins? Why does everything provoke your spirit?

Proverbs 12:16 says, "A fool shows his annoyance at once, but a prudent man overlooks an insult." I hate to say this, but many Christians are foolish because they show their annoyance immediately about so many things. The "prudent" man is the one with "discretion." He "overlooks insults." Ask yourself honestly, are you able to overlook insults and offenses? I'm telling you, it's hard to do. Christians are especially judgmental of other Christians. Somehow, we believe that they are supposed to be sinless. Whenever others fail us, we show our "annoyance at once!" Nothing escapes our critical scrutiny.

One of the best biblical stories that illustrates the power of overlooking an insult is that of Abigail with David. The story is found in 1 Samuel, Chapter 25. So many families name their daughters, "Abigail," because of this virtuous woman.

The Bible tells us that Abigail was "a woman of good understanding and beautiful appearance" (v3). We are not told why, but unfortunately for her, she was married to "Nabal," a "man who was harsh and evil in his doings" (v3). The Hebrew name, "Nabal," means "fool" or "stupid." It is translated as "fool" or "foolish" in various Psalms and Proverbs.[135] Abigail even told David, "Please, let not my lord regard this scoundrel Nabal. For as his name is, so is he: Nabal is his name, and folly is with him" (v25). I wanted to say, "Nabal is his name, and foolishness is his game!" He was an utter fool.

Nabal owned a lot of sheep – "three thousand sheep" (v2) and also "a thousand goats." Nabal had gone to Carmel with his shearers to shear his sheep. While these workers were out in the field shearing sheep, David and his soldiers decided on their own to protect the workers and their sheep from enemies who might harm them. They did this "night and day" for free.

David sent "ten young men" of his servants to Nabal to ask for food and provisions while they were fleeing from Saul. These servants came in David's name and in peace. They were merely asking for food in return for all the days of free protection by the soldiers.

Nabal treated them harshly and rejected their request. When David heard of it, "He girded up his sword" and told his people, "Every man gird on his sword" (v13). David was insulted by Nabal and he was going to kill Nabal, some of his sheep, and all his workers for this offensive rejection. Nabal was as good as dead.

Someone told Abigail what her husband had done and what David was getting ready to do. She had to hurry. Supernaturally, she quickly "took two hundred loaves of bread, two skins of wine, five sheep already dressed, five seahs of roasted grain, one hundred clusters of raisins, and two hundred cakes of figs, and loaded them on donkeys" (v18). She went to David and "dismounted quickly from her donkey, fell on her face before David, and bowed down to the ground" (v23).

---

[135] See Psalm 14:1, 39:8, 53:1, 74:18, 74:22; Proverbs 17:7, 17:21, and 30:22. This includes the famous saying, "The *fool* has said in his heart, 'There is no God.'"

She presented all these provisions to David and begged that he would forgive the "offense" of her foolish husband and "not avenge himself" (v31). David told her that she had "kept me this day from coming to bloodshed and from avenging myself with my own hand" (v33). David had plans to kill all the males that were with Nabal (v34). Just think, for one offense by a foolish man, David was going to kill a lot of people. This is the way of anger – People must restraint us lest we do a lot of damage.

It's very interesting to me that Proverbs speaks several times about "the wrath of the king," "the king's anger," and "as messengers of death is the king's wrath."[136] His anger is like the "roaring of a lion." "Whoever provokes him to anger sins against his own life" (20:2). Abigail saved her life and the lives of others, because she was a "wise woman" who knew how to "appease the anger of the king." She overcame evil with good. She showed kindness and it caused David to overlook the offense. What a powerful word for us!

Proverbs 22:24-25 – Anger is Cruel & Influential

We taught on these verses in the second chapter, *Moses and Anger.* Proverbs 22:24-25 states, "*Make no friendship with an angry man, and with a furious man do not go, lest you learn his ways and set a snare for your soul.*"

When I first met this Christian lady, I was amazed at her virtue. She was kind, patient, merciful, and humble. She spoke with a quiet, gentle voice. There was a godly attraction to her personality. When the apostle Peter spoke of "the incorruptible beauty of a gentle and quiet spirit, which is very precious in the sight of God," these words described this lady exactly. She reminded me a lot of my wife.

At the time that I met her, she was single. She had gone through a difficult divorce after her husband's multiple adulteries. She stayed single for many years and was in no rush to get married.

---

[136] See Proverbs 14:35, 16:14, 19:12, and 20:2.

About two years later, a man came into her life. He had many of the same interests in the things of the Lord as her. She slowly warmed up to him and fell in love. Within another year, they were married by a Pastor.

There was one big character flaw in him that dominated so much of his life – he was very angry. I'm not always sure why it happens, but many times, I have seen sweet, kind women marry strong-willed, loud men. There's an attraction there that is difficult to explain.

After about two years of marriage, there was a significant change in her. Gradually, she also became very angry. I saw her easily frustrated. She snapped at people. She became quick-tempered. Many things irritated her. She seemed to be on edge all the time. The sad truth is that *she became like him*. The girl who was once gentle, kind, and sweet was now bitter, angry, and irate. What an unhappy transformation.

Make no mistake about it, anger spreads. It spreads from the husband to the wife and children; it spreads from the bosses to employees; it spreads from the coach to the players. Proverbs warns us: "Don't go! Don't make friends! Stay away from angry people." Why? Because "*you will learn their ways*." They will influence your way of thinking. You will develop their bad habits. You will look like them.

More than that, angry people will "set a snare for your soul." As we taught previously, it will "put a noose" around your soul. You will be ensnared. Anger will hang you. In a subtle way, anger will slowly take the spiritual life out of you.

The wisdom of God teaches us another thing about anger: Anger is cruel. Proverbs 27:4 says, "Anger is cruel and fury overwhelming, but who can stand before jealousy?" Any good definition of "cruel" has the word, "deliberate" or "intentional" in it. Angry people deliberately choose to inflict pain and anguish against others. It's a subtle form of revenge. It's payback. It's getting even.

I remember the Christian man who received a divorce decree from his ex-wife in the mail. She intentionally waited until the day of their anniversary. She made sure it arrived on the day they were married. This is cruel.

129

I remember a worship leader who had to be corrected by his Pastor for some evil things he was doing. After the Pastor administered the rebuke, this worship leader waited until Saturday night to go to the church sanctuary. He had a key to get in. He went and removed the speakers and microphones from the church that he had donated to the church about one year earlier. He stole the equipment that now rightfully belonged to the church. When the church members arrived on Sunday morning, they had no sound system to work with. This is cruel.

I remember the Christian lady who carried her baby to full term. When she went to the hospital with her husband, the doctors told her that she would need a C-Section surgery to remove the child from her womb because the umbilical cord was wrapped around the baby's neck. Fortunately, the child survived, although she came out purple in various parts of her body. When the unsaved sister, who hated her older sister's Christianity, got pregnant out of wedlock by her boyfriend, she delivered her baby through the natural process. Within one hour of delivery, she was on the hospital phone calling her Christian sister and mocking her: "I'm not even a Christian and I had a normal delivery; where is your God? Your baby almost died. You had to have a C-Section. There's no advantage to your Christian faith. I had a better outcome than you!" She rubbed it in showing her sister no mercy. This is cruel. When people are angry, they will do many hurtful things. They look for ways of getting even.

Anger influences others. Anger is cruel to others.

Most of the angry people I have met in my life have been men, but I have met a few angry women too! Watch out! The writer says in Proverbs 21:19, "Better to dwell in the wilderness, than with a contentious and angry woman." He had written only a few verses earlier, in verse 9, "Better to dwell in a corner of a housetop, than in a house shared with a contentious woman." A few chapters later, in Proverbs 25:24, we find these words: "It is better to dwell in a corner of a housetop, than in a house shared with a contentious woman." A "contentious woman" is one who is argumentative, combative, and quarrelsome. Simply put, she is an angry woman. There will be constant fights and arguments with the husband. She will yell and scream at the kids. Nothing satisfies her. And these verses teach that a husband will go out of his way to avoid such a woman. He would rather stay in the desert or live in the attic than with her. From many years of difficult counseling, I have come to learn that husbands despise angry wives. A woman they once loved, they now feel contempt for.

I don't know why some women are so angry, but the ones I have worked with have all been physically and emotionally abused in their past. Many have been molested and violated in deep and profound ways. Many have seen their fathers or their husbands run off with other women. Such rejection generates a lot of anger. Only Jesus can heal such deep-seated wounds. May the Lord give us discernment and compassion to deal with such people. Angry people are hurting people. They are unloved. Only the love of God in Christ Jesus can restore these souls.

Now a word to women about their angry men. Here is a powerful word of wisdom – Proverbs 19:19, "A hot-tempered man must pay the penalty; if you rescue him, you will have to do it again." Ladies, mark this down: *Anger is a very difficult thing to break in a man.* And if he has been angry for a long time, you will have to "rescue" and "deliver" him "again and again." Many women get very  frustrated because they don't see any improvement in the angry disposition of their husbands. Just know, this is very common among men. There is no easy formula to deliver a man from his anger.

I remember going to the home of a man and woman who were having serious marital problems. From my opening question to the end of the meeting, it was one angry exchange after another. I don't think either of them realized how loud they were getting. At one point, the man was telling her to "shut up" as he yelled at her. "Sorry Pastor, but she really pisses me off!" the man said with a straight face.

Then the wife said this – "Pastor, this has been our daily life for over twenty years of marriage. I am constantly dealing with his angry outbursts. He controls everything and everyone. I'm tired of dealing with his anger." She added, "I have to calm him down *again and again.*"

Ladies, there is a "penalty" in living with an angry man: You will have to deal with him "again and again." Don't give up.

Continue to fight for your husband. Maybe your nerves are raw. You probably are tired physically and emotionally. Get on your knees and fight! His angry spirit will wear you down, but the Holy Spirit can never be defeated. What you can't do in your own strength, God will do by His power. When you are weak, He is strong. Trust in the Lord with all your heart and don't lean on your own understanding. This also is a word from Proverbs (3:5).

Concluding Remarks

As you can see, the Book of Proverbs says a lot about anger. There is so much material here, that it would require months of careful meditation and prayer.

Let me close with a positive word on "slow to anger." Proverbs 16:32 says, "He who is slow to anger is better than the mighty, and he who rules his spirit than he who takes a city." People who are calm and patient with others are the strongest people on earth. "Slow to anger" is a very difficult disposition to master. We live in a world that is full of anger. Bitterness is everywhere. Hatred and violence are expressed at every turn. In our culture, anger is normal. It's like breathing air.

A man or woman who is "slow to anger" has learned "to rule his spirit." They have learned the secret of self-control and contentment. Such a person is surely filled with the Holy Spirit of God. Such people are "better than the mighty" and better "than he who takes a city." A man who is slow to anger is better and stronger than a military commander and his army who can overrun a city. But those who are angry are like the person of Proverbs 25:28, "Whoever has no rule over his own spirit is like a city broken down, without walls." Cities without walls were easily conquered by enemy armies. And we will be easily overcome by temptations, demons, and habitual sins because we are out of control with our anger. May the Holy Spirit restraint your madness and work self-control in you.

Let's pray: *"Father, I see clearly from the wisdom of Your Word that anger is foolish. Anger labels us a fool. Empower me, day by day, to be "slow to anger" and not "quick-tempered." Restrain me from being easily angered and short-tempered. Lord, guard the door of my lips so that I will answer the angry man with gentle words. Defuse the hot temper in me. Today, give me a calm and patient spirit with everybody. Remove me from any situation where I might try to stir up and agitate others. Anoint me to be a peacemaker not a troublemaker. I want to overlook insults, offenses, and sins. Many things are just not worth fighting about. Help me to release and forgive others. Deliver me from a critical spirit. I desire to influence my husband/wife and children with good not evil. Remind me daily that 'anger is cruel.' May you give me a heart like Abigail, who worked to defuse the anger and not stir it up! Man's anger never works God's righteousness. May I be strong in the Lord and His mighty power. May self-control and gentleness fill my heart. As the elect of God, I will put on tender mercies, kindness, humility, meekness, and longsuffering. I will bear with others and forgive them, even as Christ has forgiven me. In the name of Jesus Christ my Lord, amen!"*

The next teaching is on Ahithophel & Anger. It is a study on revenge and anger. It is about getting even and its deadly consequences.

YouTube Videos:
- **The Christian and Anger 07a**
- **The Christian and Anger 07b**

THE CHRISTIAN & ANGER

8

Ahithophel & Anger

*"Ahithophel said to Absalom, 'I would choose twelve
thousand men and set out tonight in pursuit of David.
I would attack him while he is weary and weak. I
would strike him with terror, and then all the people
with him will flee. I would strike down only the
king.'"*
(2 Samuel 17:1-2)

Ahithophel went from gifted counselor to
revengeful conspirator because of anger that
raged out of control. *He wanted to do to David
what David had done to him.* I want to look at his life carefully,
because if there was ever someone who had a right to be angry at
another, it was Ahithophel. So often, when you're angry at
someone, you feel that because he hurt or offended you, then you
have a right to be angry. This always has tragic results. This is a
fearful verse in the Bible: "But God said to Jonah, 'Have you any
right to be angry? Do you have a right to be angry about the vine?'
'I do,' he said. 'I am angry enough to die!'"[137] Many times, anger
is all about your rights. You feel entitled to your anger.

---

[137] See Jonah 4:4, 9.

Let's examine the heart and life of a man whose anger and revenge brought about his own demise. He took matters into his own hands, and he brought sexual sin into David's life. He wanted to kill David himself. His name was Ahithophel the Gilonite. He was a great counselor, but he turned into a great conspirator.

The Power, Position & Prestige of Ahithophel

Ahithophel had everything going for him. He was the personal advisor and trusted counselor to one of the greatest kings of all time – King David. He was known as "David's counselor," or simply, "the king's counselor."[138] He was so gifted that "every word Ahithophel spoke seemed as wise as though it had come directly from the mouth of God."[139] Also, "Eliam, the son of Ahithophel the Gilonite,"[140] was a highly-decorated military leader. He was part of David's "mighty men," the top fighters in Israel. Ahithophel was sure proud of his warrior-son. This anointed counselor had another thing going for him – he had a beautiful granddaughter named "Bathsheba, the daughter of Eliam."[141] If that wasn't enough, Ahithophel's granddaughter marries another one of David's mighty men – "Uriah the Hittite."[142] So, in summary, Ahithophel has a privileged position in the kingdom; a son who was a brave warrior, and a beautiful granddaughter who married another skilled fighter. This man could walk around with his head held high! His life was prosperous and blessed. He was the envy of those around him.

The Nightmare Begins

In one moment of passionate lust, Ahithophel's picture-perfect family life came crashing down. And it was all done by

---

[138] See 2 Samuel 15:12 and 1 Chronicles 27:33.
[139] See 2 Samuel 16:23, NLT.
[140] See 2 Samuel 23:34. The warriors are in 2 Samuel 23:24-39.
[141] See 2 Samuel 11:3. In 1 Chronicles 3:5, Eliam is known as "Ammiel" and Bathsheba is called "Bathshua."
[142] See 2 Samuel 23:39 and 1 Chronicles 11:41.

his boss! David sent messengers to "take"[143] Bathsheba and bring her to the palace. He commits adultery with her and she becomes pregnant. Yes, this was adultery, but it was as close to a rape as you can get; and from someone in a position of power. Shortly thereafter, to cover up his sin, David orders Joab to put Uriah on the frontlines and to withdraw all support. Uriah is "struck down" and "killed by the sword of the Ammonites,"[144] the very enemies of God and Israel. To make matters worse, David is told by God, "You have despised Me, and taken the wife of Uriah the Hittite to be your wife."[145] Now he is married to Ahithophel's granddaughter. Beyond that, he's killed her husband and devastated her father, Eliam! David himself wrote that Ahithophel was his "companion and acquaintance, we took sweet counsel together, and walked together to the house of God."[146] Ahithophel had been violated in the worse way by his king and close friend! Ahithophel and his family have been shattered by the adultery and murder committed by King David!

To add salt to the wounds, David is not arrested nor does he go to prison to serve fifty years for his reckless behavior. Because David is the king, he's not punished by the judicial system of that day. He seems to have gotten away with it,[147] and he's taken Ahithophel's granddaughter into his own house as wife. This is not right! This is unjust! This is an outrage! Can you feel Ahithophel's pain? How would you feel if your daughter or granddaughter is raped, becomes pregnant, and her husband is murdered? Then he has the audacity to take her to be his wife, and now you have to live with him for the rest of your life in your family line. This is real pain! Ahithophel is going to have to process some fiery anger over this injustice. If it was his enemy, it would be bad enough, but it was his friend. It was his boss. It was someone who received his counsel.

---

[143] *"They took her"* indicates his messengers whisked her away by the authority of the king. She really had no say in the matter. It was not consensual. See 2 Samuel 11:4.

[144] See 2 Samuel 11:15 and 12:9.

[145] See 2 Samuel 12:10.

[146] See Psalm 55:12-14.

[147] Although God's judgment and discipline wreak havoc in David's life years later.

There is no indication from the Scriptures that Ahithophel demanded a hearing. There is no indication that he was angry at David and plotted to kill him *right away*. But there is every indication that he held it in. He was seething, raging, and burning with anger on the inside. He held it in for many years. He manifested the most common type of anger – passive-aggressive. Let's now fast-forward some years and see what he does to take matters into his own hands.

Absalom's Rebellion & Ahithophel's Revenge

In 2 Samuel, Chapter 15, we're at a very terrible period in David's life. By the judgment of God, he is paying for the sin of Uriah's murder and Bathsheba's adultery. David's own son has risen up against him. He was a monstrous, seditious, murderous, and rebellious man. His name was Absalom. David is fleeing Jerusalem with his officials. Absalom is coming from Hebron to Jerusalem to be installed as the new king.

Notice at 2 Samuel 15:12 that Ahithophel did not go to Absalom; Absalom went to Ahithophel. I think Absalom was aware of what happened with Ahithophel, and maybe a time or two, he heard Ahithophel share his grievance with others. Now notice at verse 31, that Ahithophel has gone from *counselor* to *conspirator*.[148] Ahithophel had now joined Absalom's terrible rebellion and sedition.

At last, the full strength of Ahithophel's poison and venom are clearly seen in 2 Samuel 16:20-23. *It's payback time for Ahithophel.* He's going to even the score. Ahithophel does two things: He counsels Absalom to (rape) have sex with ten of David's concubines in the sight of all Israel on the roof of the palace; and then, he's going to go after David to kill him. *The very thing that David did to him, he's going to do to David.* Proverbs 24:29 warns us: "Do not say, 'I'll do to him as he has done to me; I'll pay that man back for what he did.'" We're going

---

[148] Note that when Absalom went to get Ahithophel, and he joined the "increasing numbers," that is when "the *conspiracy* grew strong." See 2 Samuel 15:12.

to see now why "anger is one letter short of danger," and "the person who angers you, controls you."

The first sin was handled by Absalom when he had sex with the concubines, but now Ahithophel wants to take matters into his own hands. He's going to deal with David *personally*. He wants no middle man. Ahithophel's rage is in full bloom. "Ahithophel said to Absalom, 'I would choose twelve thousand men and set out tonight in pursuit of David. I will attack him while he is weary and weak. I will strike him with terror, and then all the people with him will flee. I will strike down only the king.'"[149] Notice all the "I's." Notice the personal nature of his words. He wanted David alone – "I will attack him," "I will strike him with terror," and "I will strike only the king." It has come full circle. He advises sexual sin, and then he looks for murder. The same thing that David did to him, he's doing to David.

As you know, Hushai gives advice that is accepted by Absalom and his elders above Ahithophel's advice. So let's look at the end of the story for Ahithophel. 2 Samuel 17:23 reads, "He put his house in order and then hanged himself. So he died and was buried in his father's tomb." He hangs himself. He becomes one of only five men in the Bible who committed suicide. Instead of killing David, he ended up killing himself. He never had a chance to carry out his revenge. Mark it down: Anger with revenge will hurt you more than it hurts others.

I know this is ugly, but can you picture him hanging from a noose on a branch of a tree? Can you see him swinging back and forth in the wind out in the middle of nowhere? Can you imagine what his son, Eliam, is going through, and Bathsheba his granddaughter? This is where revenge leaves people. It leaves you hanging with bitterness, unforgiveness, and anger. It kills your soul. What a terrible sight, but one that is real for us today.

---

[149] See 2 Samuel 17:1-2.

A World Filled with Pain

The world is full of Ahithophels. So many people of the world are suffering enormous pain because of injustice. People have been violated. Others have been abused. Multitudes have been taken advantage of. What must be going through the minds of people who were molested by Catholic priests? Some priests were simply moved to other parishes and violated more children. What about those 1,000s of families who lost loved ones during 9/11? What are they dealing with even today?

I remember an African-American couple who put their 11-year-old son on Flight 77 in Washington D.C. with his school teacher to fly out west. He was being honored for his academic achievements with a special trip to California. When they learned that their son died on 9/11 when the plane crashed into the Pentagon, the father, mother, and older sister laid on his bed, held hands, and cried together until the early hours of the next morning! Oh, what pain! Can you imagine the grief, sorrow, anger, and confusion that family has been processing?

What about all the families around the world that have lost loved ones due to suicide bombings in hotels, trains, schools, and markets? What about those who lived but were maimed? What about all those soldiers that have been crippled for life by IEDs in the war on terror? What about the families of Polly Klaas, Laci Peterson, and Nicole Simpson, who were violated in the worst way? And what about the affairs that have devastated men, women, and children everywhere? What about the scandalous affairs of famous people? Oh, the shame, guilt, depression, and anger that these families have walked through! These public sexual scandals have dragged these families through the sewer.

What if we were to gather those who have been shattered by all the rapes, teen pregnancies, drug overdoses, suicides, robberies, murders, kidnappings, earthquakes, tsunamis, drunk driver killings, molestations, bank failures, Enron scandals, Bernard Madoff rip-offs, industrial and traffic accidents, and those who have lost all their entire retirement savings?! *There is a lot of injustice in this world – and a lot of anger.* Ecclesiastes 4:1-2 gives us a reality check: "Again I looked and saw all the oppression that was taking place under the sun: I saw the tears of the oppressed – and they have no comforter; power was on the side of their oppressors – and they have no comforter. And I declared that the dead, who had already died, are happier than the living, who are still alive."

According to some of the best chronological studies done on 2 Samuel 11, there's about 12-13 years of time between when David committed adultery and murder (1006 B.C.), and 2 Samuel 17 when Ahithophel unleashes his anger and revenge (993 B.C.). That's a long time to be wrestling with the anger and torment of David's evil actions. Anger is like a fire. People can hold it in for a time, often for a long time, but eventually it will be unleashed. If a person does not deal with his anger through Jesus Christ, it will eat away at the very core of his being. Proverbs 27:4 says that "anger is cruel." It is cruel to the one who is angry; and it is cruel to the one on the receiving end of the anger. What kind of heaviness must surround all the people and families mentioned above? *There is a lot of anger in this world.* There are many who are enraged and want revenge.

A Great Personal Trial

Perhaps the most difficult episode in my life happened many years ago when our worship leader and I (Pastor) had a falling out. I had to process an unbelievable amount of pain, anguish, grief, and *anger.* In the providence of God, He graciously exposed many weaknesses, sins, and idols in my life. Like gold and silver, the fiery trial brought to the surface lots of scum and impurities that I didn't even know were there. In the end, it was used by the Lord to strengthen, deliver, and promote me. Like Jacob, I was left with a limp in my step.

John (not his real name) was a faithful, committed, and hard-working man. He was also a very talented worship leader. He had a lot of technical skill in sound systems, digital devices, and the incorporation of instruments for worship services. He tended to be hard on people, but perhaps this was part of his zeal for God. Moreover, he married our church secretary and bookkeeper, who was also a very gifted musician (keyboard player). Betty (not her real name) was also one of my personal intercessors and someone who I worked with nearly every day in the overall operation of the church. She was incredibly talented, honest, and hard-working. Both John and Betty worked together with others to make a powerful worship team. *And both were my close friends and a brother and sister in Christ Jesus.* We prayed and worshipped together, fellowshipped in each other's homes, and blessed each other in every way. God used our relationship to bring a lot of good to many people. I would take John and his anointed worship team to conventions where I was speaking or to joint services that I had coordinated. We were a match made in heaven – at least that's what I thought.

I can't say I understand *why* it all went wrong, but it did. While I know that the devil attacks good worship leaders, I don't want to blame him for all the troubles. There was certainly a lot of flesh *and anger.*

I began to notice that this worship leader was spending nearly all of his time during the day in the sanctuary working on the set-up of equipment, running cables, rearranging instruments, and fine-tuning mixers and speakers. He had a prosperous business that required lots of time, so why was he here at the church building every day for several hours? Why didn't he go to work? One day, I asked Betty if John's business was slowing down or if there were any problems. She told me that they had plenty of business and they were receiving many calls for work, but John would not go to the jobs, even as work orders were piling up on his desk. At that point, I knew something was wrong – seriously wrong.

The details of what happened next are still a little foggy in my mind, but when I asked him if everything was okay in his work, he became very angry. He started avoiding me and would not return my calls. Our church had a standing commitment among the leaders, that if anyone was to minister from the platform/pulpit at any service, then they needed to be in the pre-service prayer meeting. John no longer attended these prayer meetings. Because of the tension that started building between us, we both got a little testy before a Sunday morning service when I asked him why he was not in the prayer meetings. He didn't say much and walked off. During the service, he cut the morning worship service short, and he sat down abruptly in the front row of the church, right in front of where I normally teach. Needless to say, that service was very tense.

From there, things went downhill quickly. I had to remove him temporarily from leading worship until we could figure out what was happening with him. I made the serious mistake of talking to some of his in-laws, who were also in the church, just before talking to him about stepping down as worship leader. I didn't want to announce something to the whole church that they were not aware of. It was a "name withheld until notification of family." Word got back to him of these conversations. This only made matters worse. At this point, there were some angry exchanges between us over the phone. Immediately after this, he took all the sound equipment from the sanctuary that belonged to him.[150] Almost overnight, it appeared like I became his enemy and everything was then viewed with mistrust and suspicion. To make a long story short, I brought in my main leaders, and even my spiritual overseer, to try and resolve the division. Nothing worked. Matters continued to worsen. Finally, when I went to his house with another leader to try to reconcile, after about three hours of talks, he ended up asking me to leave. Further reconciliation efforts by my overseer, at my request, failed.

Shortly thereafter, he loaded onto his truck the church file cabinet that his wife had at home and dropped it off at our church office in the middle of the night. Also, by this time, rumors were swirling in the church regarding why he wasn't leading worship anymore. He "heard" that some people were accusing him of adultery. This did not happen, but I addressed the issue anyway during one of the Sunday services. He became so upset at what was happening that he angrily confronted me after one of the Sunday services in the church foyer by the kitchen. He accused me of ruining his life and he blamed me for all his problems.

That was the final straw. I was not going to go to a church where I was the Pastor and be intimated by him like this. To add fuel to the fire, he spread his grievance against me by bad

---

[150] Because of this, we later made a decision that all equipment used for church services would be owned by the church. I recommend this strongly for all churches.

mouthing me to several pastor friends. Some of them also turned against me. To this day, I have not been able to reconcile with some of them. This really angered me. I finally told him that we were putting him out of the church and he was no longer welcome. With this, he went ballistic...and it wasn't over yet!

John and Betty decided to go to another local church – but not just any church. It was the church led by a pastor friend that I had known for many years. We had even recently done a three-month discipleship course together with two other pastors.

Just when I thought we had reached the bottom of the barrel, it got worse. This church, led by my friend, never bothered to call me to find out why our worship leader and church secretary were suddenly at his church. During a Sunday morning service, some people at his church prophesied over them saying how they were right and my church and I were all wrong! Now my face was really red! I found out a few weeks later, that one of the reasons this pastor's church welcomed them was because several of his worship team members left out of division and strife to attend the church of another pastor friend! They needed help with their worship. Now the plot was thickening! And such is the sad state of many churches today – we're trying to reconcile lost people to God, and we're not even reconciled among ourselves! What hypocrisy!

During all of this, several people on the worship team and some in the congregation joined John and Betty, and they left our church and went to different churches. This was especially painful. The carnality had spread to others.

I had to address our congregation to let everyone know the decision I had to make regarding them. During a Sunday morning service, we had no worship time and we only dismissed the children to their Sunday school classes. In forty-five minutes I explained what happened and that we had put John out of the church. I tried to be very gracious in my words, but I had to be firm and take a stand.

By no means were my troubles over. They were just beginning. Besides preaching every Sunday, I now had to lead worship – and I knew nothing about sound systems, mixers, and other musical equipment. Compounding my problems, I had to take over all the bookkeeping and administration. I was pretty good with software and computers, but I had to learn the QuickBooks Accounting software overnight, and figure out how to pay all the bills, taxes, and payroll. The burden of all this was very heavy. *But God gave me supernatural grace.* I not only learned everything about sound equipment, I rewired the whole sanctuary and upgraded everything! I not only learned QuickBooks, I reprogrammed all the accounting and streamlined many functions.

But I was very angry. There was a lot of pain, hurt, offense and even unforgiveness. As if all this trouble wasn't enough, we were right in the middle of an adoption process with a little boy that was turning sour.[151] Because of the anger, which was inward, I began to have excess adrenaline in my body which made my heart race, and kept me up at night. I didn't sleep well at all. My soul was shattered. I was in trouble – and I knew it.

What was particularly painful was all the negative thinking that began to dominate my thought-life. I would relive the angry exchanges and harsh words over and over again. I could not shake these thoughts. They were with me day by day and week by week – for months. The anger I was feeling toward John would often spill over to my wife and kids. I was upset, grouchy, short with others, and very negative. I was in so much pain. I didn't understand what was happening to me. There were times when I felt like I was suffocating in my car. I would roll down the window to get air, but there was plenty of air in the car. *I saw that my soul was dying.* I kept asking God to forgive me and forgive them, but the pain in my heart didn't go away. Whenever anything bad happened, I was often confused, wondering if this is a judgment from God or an attack of the devil.

Then came the irrational fears. I knew John owned a gun. What if he went to my daughter's school and shot her? What if he started stalking me? What if he returned to the church on a Sunday and shot at me during the sermon? Strangely, I found myself going to school early to pick up my daughter *just in case*. What would I do if I saw him at a store or a Christian event in town? I thought I was going crazy. If this is what divorce was

---

[151] Praise God, this situation eventually turned around and we finally adopted my son, Daniel Elisha, three years later.

like, I realized it was hell. Talking to others about my problems brought no relief. I knew that a wounded and bitter minister would wound and embitter others. I couldn't keep going with this kind of spirit. I had no peace and no joy. Life was miserable!

Now the BIG problem – what did the Lord think about all this division and strife? All of us had failed at the most fundamental level of Christian living. We were not reconciled nor had we forgiven each other. How could I take communion? How would I preach again on reconciling with your brother? Didn't Proverbs 6:19 say that the Lord hates "a man that sows discord (stirs up dissension) among brothers?" How could I make right something that was so wrong? We had made a mess of things. Where do I even start? All of these questions haunted me.

I didn't know I was capable of such anger. In my fleshly mind, I justified reasons why I was right and he was wrong. I even had to confess to God that I hated him for what he did to me. I had never experienced that kind of honesty with God before. Here was another evil thing – *I secretly began to rejoice when I heard bad things were happening to him.* Over the course of a year or two, he lost his car, his business, his home, and his wife! She filed for divorce. I heard rumors that he was back on drugs and that he was living in a one-bedroom apartment in Arizona. Somehow, I thought, all of his troubles helped vindicate me. However, this verse in Proverbs 24:17-18, stopped me in my tracks: "Do not rejoice when your enemy falls, and do not let your heart be glad when he stumbles; lest the Lord see it, and it displease Him, and He turn away His wrath from him." I had to repent of my revengeful thoughts and feelings. I had to renounce a lot of ungodliness.

The Lord's Redemption

One day, about four or five months after everything had transpired, I went to the church building and began pacing back and forth in the front of the sanctuary. *I was discouraged, depressed, and defeated.* I lapsed into a time of extreme self-pity. I was having a good old-fashion pity party! Woe is me! No one knows the trouble I'm in! I began to feel sorry for myself. I was trying my best, but nothing was working out for me. I was looking for sympathy but receiving none.

Into this moment of darkness and despair, the Lord spoke these words directly into my heart – "You can sit there and feel sorry for yourself or you can turn everything over to Me and I will redeem it! What was meant for evil I can turn around for good. I am your Redeemer. The very thing that walked out of this church in worship, I'm going to bring right back into your very home." *That word completely delivered me from my self-pity and depression.* I can't explain how, but when I left the sanctuary that day, I knew that I was to take my young daughter to get piano lessons. I knew that I knew. Then, by the grace of God, three amazing things happened.

First, my daughter learned to play the piano and keyboard. By the time she was 10 years old, she began to lead worship from the keyboard in church services, and she would accompany me to different speaking engagements and play songs before I spoke. Suddenly, after a few years, she began to write songs of worship and even beautiful instrumental pieces that I've never heard before. Leah also picked up the guitar, and after a few weeks of practice, began to play it like she had been playing for years. She also began writing songs of worship for guitar. Technically, she can do amazing things on the keyboard and guitar. She has unbelievable gifting and grace to do what she does. It's true, *the very gift of leading worship and playing keyboard that walked out of my church came right into my home!* Leah now understands that her main call in life is to be a worship leader. God is good!

Second, after much prayer and soul-searching, the Lord allowed my wife and I to reconcile with Betty. We humbled ourselves, went to her, and asked for forgiveness. Eventually, we even hired her to help us with our year-end accounting and to help train our current bookkeeper! God turned it all the way around so that now she could be a blessing to us. Gone were all the hurtful feelings and pain (for me). I tell you, reconciliation is a huge blessing! The Latin word "reconcile" basically means "turning an enemy into a friend." That is what God has done with us through Jesus Christ according to 2 Corinthians 5:17-21. The "ambassadors for Christ" of these verses are those who have "been given the ministry of reconciliation" and the "message of

THE CHRISTIAN & ANGER

reconciliation." *The only reason we can be reconciled to Betty is because we have been reconciled to Christ.* Sadly, I never reconciled with John because he passed away a few years later.

Third, the Lord anointed and called me into an intercessory ministry for John and others. My lifeline was Matthew 5:44 – "But I say to you, love your enemies, bless those who curse you, do good to those who hate you, and *pray for those who spitefully use you and persecute you.*" It was the early church father, Tertullian, who wrote, "To love friends is the custom for all people, but to love enemies is customary only for Christians." Initially, I had trouble praying any kind of blessing on John. I wanted him cursed! I didn't want anything good to happen to him; I wanted bad things for him. Such was my secret life of revenge. But the more I prayed, and the more I blessed him, the more God healed my heart of bitterness, anger, and revenge. I actually began to take great joy in praying for him. The truth is, on the cross, Jesus paid for all those sins that were done towards me or all those wrongs that came my way unjustly. After what happened with John, I trained myself to immediately begin praying earnestly for anyone who hurts or offends me. *If a Pastor is to survive in today's ministry environment, he must be quick to forgive and pray.* Unforgiveness only makes you bitter. Every week, sometimes every day, I find myself praying and blessing John. *You swallow up bitterness, anger and revenge as you pray for your enemies.* Nothing else really works.

Dealing with Anger and Revenge

Revenge takes place when we pay back evil for evil. Romans 12:17, 19 says, "Do not repay anyone evil for evil. Do not take revenge, my friends, but leave room for God's wrath, for it is written: 'It is mine to avenge; I will repay,' says the Lord." Evil is overcome by good. If you try to take matters into your own hands, you will end up with lots of anger and revenge. This will have devastating consequences on your life. Don't let your enemies make you bitter. War against it. They want you to become like them. Refuse it. If they throw a poison dart at your heart, don't throw it back. Nasty words are like swords and knives. They cut, injure and hurt. *If you're bitten by a snake, don't become one.*

The apostle Peter learned this valuable lesson in 1 Peter 3:9-11: "Do not repay evil with evil or insult with insult, but with blessing, because to this you were called so that you may inherit a blessing. For, 'Whoever would love life and see good days must keep his tongue from evil and his lips from deceitful speech. He must turn from evil and do good; he must seek peace and pursue it.'" One of the most important things I learned from my experience with John and Betty is if you want to "see good days you must keep your tongue from evil." That tongue can cause great harm! Proverbs 13:3 is a powerful verse: "He who guards his mouth guards his life, but he who opens wide his lips shall have destruction!" *When you are offended, talk to God.* Don't talk to others and spread gossip. That's exactly what the devil wants. His very name means "slanderer." He is a malicious gossiper. Don't join him! I committed the grave sin of opening wide my mouth against John and Betty, and I reaped a great deal of destruction. God's Word is true. It will happen. We are called to bless others, not curse them.

Paul wrote in 1 Thessalonians 5:15, "Make sure that nobody pays back wrong for wrong, but always try to be kind to each other and to everyone else." It's hard to be kind when others are cruel. Wasn't it Jesus who said in Matthew 5:38: "You have heard that it was said, 'Eye for eye, and tooth for tooth.'" That's revenge – "eye for an eye." This is what Ahithophel did. This is "evil for evil." In the next verse, the Lord says, "But I tell you, do not resist an evil person. If someone strikes you on the right cheek, turn to him the other also." This is overcoming evil with good. Remember: Humility prevails over pride, love over hate, and good over evil.

Solomon warns us in Proverbs 20:22, "Do not say, 'I'll pay you back for this wrong!' Wait for the LORD, and He will deliver you." It's very hard to wait on the Lord when others have wronged you. But this verse has the promise of God – "He will deliver you." And His deliverance will be mighty. He can overrule the decisions and actions of all men – good or evil. Proverbs 24:29 reads, "Do not say, 'I'll do to him as he has done to me; I'll pay that man back for what he did.'" We want others to feel the same pain that we're feeling. Somehow, we deceive ourselves into thinking that "paying back" really hurts the other person. Actually, it really hurts us – and makes us bitter. Don't become another Ahithophel. Again, Proverbs 25:21-22, "If your enemy is hungry, give him bread to eat; and if he is thirsty, give him water to drink; for so you will heap coals of fire on his head, and the Lord will reward you." Kindness towards an enemy seems out of place, but the Lord will reward you. You will not be a doormat or taken advantage of – you will be blessed by God! Interestingly, the great commandment of the OT was "Do not seek revenge or bear a grudge against one of your people, but love your neighbor as yourself. I am the LORD" (Leviticus 19:18).

The apostle Peter said of Jesus in 1 Peter 2:23 (NLT): "He did not retaliate when He was insulted, nor threaten revenge when He suffered. *He left His case in the hands of God, who always judges fairly.*" Forsake your anger and revenge. Leave your case in God's hands.

YouTube Videos:
- **The Christian and Anger 08a**
- **The Christian and Anger 08b**

THE CHRISTIAN & ANGER

Chapter 1 Study Questions

The author says that "anger is everywhere" and that "all of us have expressed anger." Why is anger the most common negative emotion expressed by people?

As you read the story of Jim and Linda, what were some of the relational and family dynamics going on between this couple?

Why did the Lord accept Abel's offering and reject Cain's? And how did this lead to Cain's anger and depression?

The author says that "anger is a choice. The reason many of us are angry right now is that we chose to be angry." Explain this statement.

As you look at Genesis 4:1-10 and 1 John 3:12, how is it that people like Cain do evil acts, end up blaming others, and express anger against them?

Chapter 2 Study Questions

Summarize in your own words what happened in Moses' family line through his forefather, Levi. See especially Genesis 34 and Jacob's prophecy in Genesis 49.

Review some of the events in this chapter that made Moses angry. Why was Moses the angriest man in the Bible, and highlight one of these events and explain what provoked him to anger.

We ask the question in this chapter about how should a Christian leader handle injustice and disobedience. What are some key things that should be done to avoid anger and walk in God's righteousness?

In your own words, how would you characterize Karen's life, and how would you have handled her situation if you were the Pastor?

Chapter 3 Study Questions

Elaborate on why Matthew 5:21 "reveals that it is possible to commit murder without committing the physical act. You can 'murder' someone in your heart with anger and hatred."

In your own life, how have you seen that anger is "dangerous?" Give two examples in your life or the lives of others.

Why are broken relationships in our past the root of so much anger? And why is reconciliation the answer to so much bitterness and anger in our lives?

Using Matthew 5:25-26, why does anger have such a heavy cost?

As you read Matthew 5:27-30, how are anger and adultery related spiritually?

Chapter 4 Study Questions

How is it that Samson could be the strongest man who ever lived, and yet, he could not control his anger?

Of the many superhuman feats that Samson did, which one stands out to you? Why?

The author writes that it wasn't his physical size that made Samson strong, but the Holy Spirit. Do you agree with this statement? Why or why not?

What are some steps that the man who had been married for thirty years and lived a secret life of sexual sin could have taken to break free from his bondage?

Do you agree that after the Holy Spirit, a man's greatest comforter is his wife? Explain.

Chapter 5 Study Questions

Why is it that when so many Christians sin, they want mercy; but when others sin, they want judgment?

Explain the author's comment that Jonah "was burning in anger because he was lacking in mercy."

What kind of people were the ancient Ninevites, and how does this heighten Jonah's negative feelings toward them?

Read Jonah Chapter 4 carefully. Explain how the Lord dealt with his anger.

Chapter 6 Study Questions

As you read Galatians Chapter 5, how and why is the Holy Spirit God's ultimate answer to our anger problems?

Colossians and Ephesians teach us to "put off anger." In practical terms, exactly how does a Christian do this?

Explain what the author means when he writes that "the only one who can fix you is the One who made you."

As you read Ephesians 4:26-32, what are some keys that Paul gives us for dealing with our anger?

Chapter 7 Study Questions

What did Solomon mean in Ecclesiastes 7:9 when he wrote, "For anger rests in the bosom of fools?"

In the story of the man who began to throw porcelain plates against the wall to frighten his wife, what was this man trying to accomplish? Why would this so-called Christian resort to such measures?

In your own words, explain what Proverbs 22:24-25 is saying about anger.

Proverbs 19:11 says, "The discretion of a man makes him slow to anger, and his glory is to overlook a transgression." Practically speaking, what does discretion have to do with calming anger? Describe a time when you had to "overlook a transgression" to deal with someone.

Chapter 8 Study Questions

The author writes, "Ahithophel wanted to do to David what David had done to him." How would you have dealt with David if you found out he had impregnated your granddaughter and killed her husband?

How did Ahithophel and Absalom work together to try to ruin King David?

As you read through the author's account of his problems with the worship leader, John, what would you have done differently in this circumstance?

How is the truth that God is our Redeemer the answer to our problems and troubles that are beyond our control?

What was the author trying to say when he wrote, "If you're bitten by a snake, don't become one?"

THE CHRISTIAN & ANGER

About the Author

Charlie Avila is the Senior Pastor of Clovis Christian Center in Fresno, California. He is married to Irma and has two adult children – Leah (husband: Jose) and Daniel. Pastor Charlie is the Bible teacher of the Spirit of Wisdom and Revelation teaching newsletters and the principal teacher on the Teacher of the Bible website.

He is an instructor with the Fresno School of Mission and other ministry schools. He has spoken in conferences locally, nationally, and internationally. He teaches special seminars on various Bible subjects and verse by verse studies through Old Testament and New Testament books. He has written several books available on Amazon including *The Christian and Anger*, *The Christian and Homosexuality*, *The Christian and Hell*, *The Christian & Witchcraft*, *Detecting & Dealing with False Teachings*, *Healing the Sick*, *How to Become a Christian*, *The End Times*, *Making Disciples One on One*, *Having Sex with Your Boyfriend*, *Witnessing to Jehovah's Witnesses* and various commentaries on books of the Bible including Esther, 2 Peter, and Jude. He also has many books in Spanish by the same titles as the English versions.

He can be contacted at teacherofthebible@gmail.com or Clovis Christian Center, 3606 N. Fowler Ave, Fresno, CA 93727-1124.

The videos teachings for each chapter of this book are available on YouTube. Just type "The Christian and Anger 01a Pastor Charlie Avila" (all the way through 01b, 02a, 02b, 03a, 03b…etc.) on the search line or type "teacher of the Bible" and subscribe. The videos are also available at www.teacherofthebible.com.

THE CHRISTIAN & ANGER

Selected Bibliography
(By Author)

Achtemeier, Elizabeth, *Minor Prophets I*, New International Biblical Commentary, Hendrickson Publishers, Peabody, Massachusetts.

Aitken, Kenneth T., *Proverbs*, The Daily Study Bible Series, The Westminster Press, Philadelphia.

Alexander, T. Desmond (on Jonah), *Obadiah, Jonah, Micah*, Inter-Varsity Press, Downers Grove, Illinois.

Allen, Leslie, C., *The Books of Joel, Obadiah, Jonah, and Micah*, The New International Commentary on the Old Testament, Eerdmans Publishing Company, Grand Rapids, Michigan.

Anderson, Neil T. and Rich Miller, *Getting Anger Under Control*, Harvest House Publishers, Eugene, Oregon.

Barclay, William, *The Gospel of Matthew*, Volume 1, Revised Edition, The Daily Study Bible Series, The Westminster Press, Philadelphia, Pennsylvania.

Boice, James Montgomery, *The Minor Prophets, Volume 1, Hosea – Jonah*, An Expositional Commentary, Baker Books, Grand Rapids, Michigan.

Brown, William P., *Obadiah through Malachi*, Westminster Bible Companion (WBC), Westminster John Knox Press, Louisville, Kentucky.

Campbell, D. Ross, M. D. with Rob Suggs, *How to Really Love Your Angry Child*, Life Journey, Colorado Springs, Colorado.

Carson, D. A., *Jesus' Sermon on the Mount*, An Exposition of Matthew 5-10, Baker Books, Grand Rapids, Michigan.

Chapman, Gary, *Anger: Handling a Powerful Emotion in a Healthy Way*, Northfield Publishing, Chicago, Illinois.

Cosgrove, Mark P. Ph.D., *Counseling for Anger*, Volume 16, Resources for Christian Counseling, Word Publishing, Dallas, Texas.

Davis, Dale Ralph, *Such a Great Salvation*, Exposition of the Book of Judges, Baker Book House, Grand Rapids, Michigan.

Elwell, Walter A., *Exegetical Dictionary of Theology*, Baker Book House, Grand Rapids, Michigan.

Ferguson, Sinclair B., *Man Overboard! The Story of Jonah*, The Banner of Truth Trust, Carlisle, Pennsylvania.

Ferguson, Sinclair B., *The Sermon on the Mount*, The Banner of Truth Trust, Carlisle, Pennsylvania.

Hawkins, O. S., *Jonah: Meeting the God of the Second Chance*, Loizeaux Brothers, Neptune, New Jersey.

Horton, Stanley M., *Genesis*, World Library Press, Inc., Springfield, Missouri.

Limburg, James, *Hosea – Micah*, Interpretation: A Bible Commentary for Teaching and Preaching, John Knox Press, Atlanta, Georgia.

Lloyd-Jones, D. Martyn, *Studies in the Sermon on the Mount*, Eerdmans Publishing, Grand Rapids, Michigan.

Newman, B. M. and Stine, P. C., *A Handbook on the Gospel of Matthew* from the United Bible Societies Handbook Series, Swindon, England.

Perkins, Bill, *When Good Men Get Angry*, Tyndale House Publishers, Carol Stream, Illinois.

Robinson, George L., *The Twelve Minor Prophets*, Baker Book House, Grand Rapids, Michigan.

Simonetti, Manlio, *Ancient Commentary on Scripture, Matthew 1-13*, Volume 1a, InterVarsity Press, Downers Grove, Illinois.

Stott, John R. W., *The Message of the Sermon on the Mount*, The Bible Speaks Today Series, InterVarsity Press, Downers Grove, Illinois.

Stuart, Douglas, *Hosea – Jonah*, Word Biblical Commentary, Volume 31, Word Books Publisher, Waco, Texas.

Tasker, R. V. G., *The Gospel According to Matthew*, Tyndale New Testament Commentaries, Eerdmans Publishing.

Wiersbe, Warren W., *Be Loyal (Matthew): Following the King of Kings*, Be Series Commentary, David C. Cook Publishing, Colorado Springs, Colorado.

THE CHRISTIAN & ANGER

Scriptural Reference Index

Made in the USA
Middletown, DE
06 July 2022